THE REAL MIND CONTROL

A book that will make you understand **Neuro-Linguistic** Programming

- Convince people effectively
- Become the best sales-person
- Make people think what you want them to think

RAFAEL GURKOVSKY

Want to read more exciting stories for FREE?

Join my **V.I.P** List now!

I regularly GIVEAWAY FREE books and SPECIAL DISCOUNTS!

Join my mailing list and be one of thousands we already receiving FREEBIES!

Join by visiting this site:

http://www.ravenspress.com/freeselfhelp/

Or Scan this QR Code from your smartphone to go the website directly

RAVENS PRESS

ISBN-13: 978-1519265388

ISBN-10: 1519265387

http://www.ravenspress.com/freeselfhelp/

Table of Contents

Introduction

I want to thank you and congratulate you for downloading the book, "Neuro-Linguistic Programming: The Art of Opening up New Ideas."

Though you may not be aware of it, some of the ways that you communicate may actually already be using this technique. If you are, and this is purely by accident, imagine what you could achieve if you performed many of the tasks shown within this book which strengthen your power to communicate. The mind is a vast fountain of untapped into knowledge and guidance that NLP helps you to reach.

Behind public speaking, learning to make friends and acquaintances in social and business settings is ranked one of the most stressful situations to be in. It's not that you don't want to make friends. It's just starting or joining a conversation with people you probably don't know causes you to break out in a cold sweat. If you can bring yourself to join in, you worry about making a fool of yourself instead of making new friends. The funny thing is, with a little bit of effort and learning some new skills, learning to develop rapport with other people becomes pretty simple. When I say building rapport, what I mean is simply learning how to get along with others and getting them to like you more easily. Without the ability to get along with someone though, none of the tools I'm going to outline in this book will be of any help, or at least in any lasting way. Sure, you could use them to manipulate people to get what you want, but if it's not in the best interest of the other person, it'll eventually catch up to you. Plus, it's unethical.

If you're just trying to learn how to be more comfortable in social settings, this book can help. Knowing how to read the mood of other people can go a long way in developing rapport with them. It can also help lower your stress levels by letting you have more control over the flow of the conversation.

Or maybe you picked up this book because you've tried to persuade a potential client to sign on with you but couldn't develop any kind of rapport with them. Or even worse, you turned them off personally which in turn made them uninterested in your company. Having access to the techniques I discuss in this book could help keep that from happening again. With that said, let's get started.

There is much to learn. Each person's universe is only as large as they allow it to be. By opening up a technique which embraces the thoughts and ideas of others, you are able to live a much richer life and begin to think "outside of the box." NLP allows you to do that. It's designed for everyone to use, from business people to health workers, from individuals looking for guidance to you, the reader. Everyone can use this system's tool to make their lives a richer and more rewarding place to be.

Thanks again for downloading this book, I hope you enjoy it!

Chapter 1 -What is Neuro-Linguistic Programming

"Free your expectation of the future from the grip of past failure."
John Seymour

You don't have to understand technicalities to grasp that the three words put together have some kind of meaning. Neuro means that which is of the brain, linguistic means emanating from language. Programming simply means being able to control the level of communication within set parameters that make your life easier.

Simply stated, the word Neuro comes from the word "Neurology" and points to the reality that all our actions start from our perception of our senses as processed by the brain. People are able to use their senses. The senses respond to a stimuli and when it does, what you see is a reaction that can be pleasurable or dis-pleasurable, depending upon the negativity or positivism of the event.

You need to remember that the things that you say are not merely in oral form. Your body, for example, can say a lot just by using body language and gesticulating. If you point a fist at someone, then they would get the impression you are being aggressive, just as if you embrace someone, you are being affectionate.
Where it gets a little tricky is when you introduce the word "programming" because people automatically think that you mean instilling some kind of auto response and that's a little farfetched.

The programming comes from beliefs and truths. For example, people are programmed to shake hands. It's an accepted form of greeting in society. They are programmed not to spit in public as it is not considered polite. However, if you widen the scope of that belief system, you are able to encompass other programmed events which will help enhance your approach to life and what you can achieve within it. As people grow or change their lives, they also change the programmed patterns of their lives. This involves embracing new things. That is why people say that those who are widely traveled are more conversant with neuro linguistic programming techniques because they are indeed incorporated every time an environment is changed and travelers change environment frequently.

Therefore, everyone is capable of acquiring a new expertise and that includes learning the benefits of Neuro-linguistic programming. If you want more proof, consider answering the following questions:
There are various questions which could be posed which would give a clue as to how open minded a person is. For example:

How many different varieties of weeds are there?
How many ways can you barbecue chicken?
Are you able to count the number of stars on any one given night?

All of these questions have variable answers. Thus, problems may be presented in the same manner but with neuro-linguistic programming knowledge, you are able to see more ways to answer them, rather than limiting your answers to that which you perceive to be the only possible answer from your perspective.

When you put two people together in a room and ask them what they recall about that room once they have been removed, each will see different things. This is because each perspective is different. In the same way, the questions asked above would be answered from a very narrow perspective of what you have seen or know, rather than giving a universal answer which is definitive. By giving that limited answer, you hold yourself back from seeing the wider picture which is available for everyone but that many miss.

Neuro Linguistic Programming finds its roots in the 1970s. John Grindler who was a linguistics expert, got together with Richard Bandler and the combination of expertise allowed them to look into behavioral patterns based on Gestalt theory. In fact, their adventure into this unknown was to give scope for many professions to key into the idea that success levels can be determined by the approach and the wideness of the approach helps to build the appropriate level of success.

Richard Bandler had an active interest in psychotherapy and worked hand in hand with two successful psychotherapists of that time, Fritz Perls and Virginia Satir who seemed to be using the same kind of open approach as Richard Bandler and John Grinder were seeing as advantageous.

Thus Neuro-Linguistic Programming was the next step and following studies using hypnotherapy, these pioneers found that useful therapeutic patterns were being formed which could be used to help people develop their lives, both in the area of self-help and for teaching, coaching, business application and mental help.

The systems which are used are taught by people who have qualified in teaching the methods and have experience in putting the methods into useful application within the world. Colleges exist all over the world and the learning which is done in these institutions has been proven as useful in many areas of business and personal life.

Thus, it has been established that Neuro-Linguistic approach works very well and that those who learn it are able to see things from other viewpoints and thus are able to make decisions with wider implications and more efficient results. Psychotherapists who have used this system find that their patient doctor rapport is opened up and that patients are more likely to respond well, by being taught to see the bigger picture.

Those in business can set goals higher simply because Neuro Linguistic Programming approach is able to expand the view of the worker so that the goals aimed at become very easy to expand upon. Sports people who are coached in Neuro Linguistic Programming techniques are able to push their bodies further and thus gain more expertise in their performance. So powerful is this system that it is all encompassing and of use to everyone who learns it.

History

Neuro-linguistic programming was founded by Richard Bandler and John Grinder during the 1970s. Bandler holds a BA degree in philosophy and psychology from the University of California and an MA degree in psychology from the Lone Mountain College. Grinder holds a BA degree in psychology from the University of San Francisco and a PhD in linguistics from the University of California.

The early beginnings of NLP were based on their partnership at the University of California. Bandler, then a student at the University, approached Grinder to discuss topics about modeling Gestalt therapy. The discussion became intense sessions with their peers. Soon, they were able to create an eclectic combination of the works of Fritz Perls on Gestalt therapy, Virginia Satir on hypnosis and Milton Erickson on psychiatry.

Both founders discovered that the combination of the work of Perls, Satir and Erickson created a powerful structure that has the potential to make leaps and bounds in the field of communication, development and therapy. It also has the capacity to affect a wide range of aspects in a person's personal, psychological, professional and social life. This combination was documented and codified into the NLP core principles of today.

The impetus for the founders in developing NLP was their observation of people and their performance. They found out that people, who shared similar backgrounds in education, training and experience, were performing ion a wide range of levels. Some were effective and succeeding, while some where ineffective and failing. The wide discrepancy must be caused by something that traditional studies on the successful person's background may have overlooked. They theorized that those people who are effective must have a secret or a source for their success that cannot be found in their education or experience.

The founders compiled the individual strategies and techniques employed by successful people. From this compilation, they aimed to achieve three things: discover the common threads aside from their education and experiences; condense the patterns and check for validity and finally and most importantly, share the patterns so as others can simulate them to create the same success.

The result of the compilation presented them with the one noticeable factor that differentiated those who were successful from those who were not: the quality of their communication. They discovered that successful people communicated in a different way, such as the way they talk, the words they use and even the non-verbal communication they utilized. When they simulated the communication techniques, they were able to create models that will later become the foundations of NLP.

NLP occupies a special niche in the therapeutic industry. Most therapies and interventions are focused on the problem a person had or is currently encountering. Traditional methods dissect, analyze and focus on the problem. In fact, the bulk of counseling sessions are is devoted to understanding the problem. NLP is unique in the sense that it is more solution-focused than problem-focused. Instead of a lengthy discussion of how the problem came about, NLP offers immediate, customized and sustainable solutions for those who practice it. This is also one of the reasons why NLP is gaining worldwide acceptance, most people do not have the luxury of time to understand a problem. They would rather devote what free time they have towards the building of a solution.

NLP is also unique because it is not a theory in the full sense of the word. Instead, it is a collection of tools that are used by those who were already successful in their fields. Instead of offering abstract ideas that may never be translated into actual practice, NLP gives you the actual tools ready for you to use. It also has the potential to link both your conscious and unconscious thoughts and resources, allowing you to make a better assessment of your potential.

Rewards
Success is one of the most immediate rewards of NLP. There is virtually no limit to the reach of NLP in your life; it can be personal, professional, social, financial, spiritual, health and general well-being. Through NLP you can achieve personal success in the form of confidence and unlearning bad habits. Professional success can also be gained through job promotions and effective selling. Social success, such as with relationships and sensitivity, is also made possible.

Financial success can be achieved when you are more in control of your decisions on earning, spending and saving. You can have a better or a more positive outlook in life enriching your spirituality. Health choices become improved and sustained.

Another set of rewards to those who practice NLP are those found in the path towards success. You develop better management skills, feel more motivated and enthusiastic and you can make sound and well-thought of decisions. You can identify, address, accept or surpass your limitation. You can make yourself more receptive by opening your minds towards new learning and beliefs. You develop coping skills to everyday stresses in life.

Perhaps, the most important reward of NLP is that you are able to change from within. Sometimes, people overestimate the effect of the outside world to them. They think that they are forever bound by the will of those around them. In fact, instead of the world affecting you, the truth is that you affect the world. The promotion you may have missed is not because of the decision of top management but because you projected a lack of confidence or failed in asserting yourself among your colleagues. This passivity is what caused the top management to choose another person over you.

When you retake control of yourself and change yourself from within, you can exude the change in your immediate environment. From there, the world will change in your favor. Of course, changing yourself from within is easier said than done. The changes cannot be done overnight and it must not be done haphazardly. Unguided, the change you make may prove disadvantageous to you down the road. NLP provides the map through which you can change yourself towards your true development and improvement.

Chapter 2 – Understanding the Basics

The first key to understanding NLP can be found ion the keywords of its name. The basic principle of NLP is that the connection of the neurological system in your body (neuro), to the language that you use, both verbal and non-verbal (linguistic) can affect the behavioral **patterns you use to achieve your goals (programming).**

Neurology:
Neurology refers to the working of the human nervous system. Before we focus on that, we need to first look at the components of the nervous system, mainly the central nervous system- dealing with the direct acts of thinking, storing and compartmentalizing information and planning and implementing actions- and the peripheral nervous system, which is responsible for the reflexive actions taken in sudden, unexpected situations, which do not require pre-processed thoughts.

The nervous system of a person is the tool used by the body to experience the world outside of it and then process it inside the mind. The system makes use of the five major senses: auditory, gustatory, kinesthetic, olfactory and visual. By using the ears, tongue, skin and motion, nose and eyes, the internal mind can process the external world.

Let us have a look now at how the CNS functions. The CNS is the root of all of a human's ideas, judgment and perception. When in a situation, our central nervous system analyzes the situation it finds itself in, and based on either two of the following it executes certain actions, making our body respond in particular ways:

• Based on previous experiences: Experiences which are stored in our brain can be called upon, to guide the mind in taking decisions in similar seeming situations.

• Based on the surrounding environment: In cases where there is no prior experience of an event, the human brain conjures up a solution which is deeply rooted in the bringing up which we have gone through, and the environment the human being has been subjected to.

•As is evident, everything from experiences to environment gets stored in the human brain, and affects our way of thinking. Due to this, two humans going through similar situations may find themselves employing entirely different approaches on how to go about handling said situation.

This variance arises mainly due to the difference in perception.

It thus becomes important to be able to compartmentalize and retrieve this information in an efficient, effective manner. NLP helps us in doing just that.

Language:
Linguistics is the second parameter in NLP. In primitive terms, linguistics is the study of language. Here, it refers to the medium adopted to convey our thoughts into actions and to express our views. Though it may sound over-hyped, language is probably the most important part of having an effective and realistic goal achieving.

The formation of the language that a person uses is based on the result of the processed information of the senses. Meaning and interpretation are given to for information from the auditory sense as sound, gustatory as taste, kinesthetic as feeling, olfactory as smell and visual as images. These interpretations are then expressed through language, both verbal and non-verbal.

One of the major drawbacks people face today is that of miscommunication. They are unable to express their views clearly, and even they attempt, they end up speaking before thinking. This oftentimes leads to a mixed reaction from the recipient of the message, and hence hinders the efficiency of the mind of the sender. While this pertains to external communication, the same importance must be given to internal communication, as there is a continuous and constant monologue ongoing in the background of the human mind, be it while decision making, or while comprehending a situation. For this reason, internal communication needs to be clear, comprehensive and precise.

Programming:
Once the mind and our linguistics have been optimized to achieve full results, they need to be coordinated together, in order to train the mind to work in the best possible way, which is done through programming, and having control command over our mind & language.

The first step is to organize our thoughts, feelings and ideas, in order to increase the efficiency of the brain. As the saying goes "A cluttered mind is the devil's workshop"! A clutter in the storage room of the body can lead to unwanted, undesirable emotional outburst at inconvenient times, thereby obstructing the efficiency of a person, in either professional or personal fields.

It is here where programming helps by keeping in control the emotions, disallowing them to interfere in a particular situation where it is not required. It so happens sometimes, that due to an overload of information the human brain can also sometimes get confused on how to produce the exact information required in a situation. In such a case, programming helps by compartmentalizing and categorizing stored information, so that information retrieval can be optimized.

The programming is the total result of the way you organize your thoughts, ideas and actions from the interpretation of your senses and made obvious by your language. It will be expressed in your behavior, which causes changes in the outside world.

For example, an employee is on his desk that is stacked with paperwork that needs to be processed and reported the next day.

His senses are bombarded by stimuli, hearing his boss tell him how urgently he needs the tasks done and seeing the clock tick away minute by minute. He then takes a deep breath and tells his co-worker that he can never finish the work on time. After all of his co-workers leave, he tells himself that his task is a lost cause and he might as well give up, go home and leave the work unfinished. At the end of his overtime shift, he does fail to complete his task and goes home.

The idea behind NLP is that the employee could have been successful in his task if he had approached his situation in a different state of mind and in with a different set of language. Instead of feeling defeated, his state of mind should have been that of victory and achievement. Instead of using words that preempt failure, he should have used language that is anticipative of success. In NLP, it is neither the clock nor the amount of work that caused the failure, but the employee himself or more specifically his behavior as a result of his state of mind and use of words.

The success therefore can be achieved not on initially changing the world outside, but on changing the world within you. By retaking control of how you interpret the data provided by your sensory organs and how you put into words these interpretations, you can program yourself with an appropriate or desired behavior. When you have changed your behavior as a result of changes in your inner world, the external world around you will change as a consequence of it.

The Three Levels of Mind:
Our mind consists of three parts: the conscious mind, the subconscious mind and the unconscious mind. The conscious mind is the current state of awareness, of the surroundings and the information pertaining to it. This data is readily accessible for use by the mind. The subconscious mind stores information which can be reached and retrieved with some level of difficulty. The information getting stored in the subconscious gets interpreted continuously by the brain, but the

brain isn't actively aware of this.

This concept will be better explained through an example. When we find ourselves in a known environment, we automatically reach out without paying specific attention the environment, and conduct ourselves in a familiar manner. Similarly, when we speak in our native tongue, the words come automatically, without us having to put an extra effort to conjure those words.

Finally, the unconscious mind, which is responsible for our instincts, and those feelings we attribute to our gut instinct. This information, stored in the unconscious mind, isn't available as freely as the information stored in the conscious or the subconscious. Though it is unknown to us, it nevertheless affects our actions, as well as impulsive decision making.

NLP helps retrieve and access the data stored in the unconscious, by making a collection of facts based on past experiences, forming a data bank, and eventually making the information stored in the unconscious a part of the subconscious and finally the conscious mind.

The Common Occurrence Neuro Linguistics Programing High Stress Jobs:

Some professions such as medical legal, security etc. require extreme high levels of energy and effort. Anytime an emergency case pops up, people have to report at all odd hours of the day and always be on their toes. Hence, during downtime, it is important these people working in these sectors maintain a cool peace of mind, as loss of focus on the job can have drastic, disastrous consequences. It is easier to lose focus as the brain is always in a state of over-work and tension.
In such cases, even while the person is resting, the unconscious mind exists in a state of anticipation, and this eventually leads to a mental breakdown among people working in such situations. NLP helps to avoid such undesirable situations by letting people take control of their own minds. It helps in dealing with their routine tasks in a much smoother way, hence enabling them to coordinate their personal and professional lives better

Planning Jobs:
Jobs such as business, marketing and engineering, which require a lot of planning, reap a lot of benefits by employing NLP trained minds. Having a vision and working towards it, with fortitude, is the prerequisite for NLP, thus it proves helpful to the people working in these fields, as it is also a job requirement in such professions. Long term projects require responsible decision making, which is one of the quality qualities developed by NLP.

Creative Jobs:

The basic foundation of NLP is to break preconceived notions thereby making the mind more flexible. This quality comes in handy when the person is employed in a field requiring creative expertise, like that of a painter, writer or actor. When NLP is practiced, the mind becomes willing to take risks and is also determined to convert these risks into rewards. New ideas emerge automatically when all three levels of the mind have been accessed completely. Additionally, the interpretation of these ideas does not require a lot of effort, as in the case of un-trained minds.

Social Life:

As important as personal and professional life can be, a person's social life matters equally in today's world. New people offer opportunities for new experiences and exploring uncharted territories also boosts up our self-esteem. Different people move in different social circles, some large, some not as much. But just having a large social circle does imply that a person is handling it well. It is important to be able to manage one's social circle in the most efficient, yet amiable manner possible, in a way that it interferes neither with one's personal life nor with a professional.

A chaotic social life is a bane in disguise of a boon. NLP improves our communication, as it is important to voice our opinions, but not at the cost of belittling the voices of others. The key is to strike a balance between our confidence and humility. NLP trains our mind to recognize and maintain this sense of balance. Also, stereotyping and generalizing are two of the biggest obstacles needed to be overcome while building a healthy social life. NLP imparts the character of open mindedness which helps in the long run while creating a healthy society.

Relationships:

Nowadays, relationships are getting harder to manage, owing to the humdrum of commotion in the human mind, as well as impatience and the tendency to give up displayed by most people. This leads to disastrous cases of estrangement, divorces, separation among families, etc. Oftentimes, all communications within a family becomes null, as it only leads to further misunderstandings and divide. NLP adds the much required discipline needed to avoid such conflicts, to our lives, by urging the unconscious mind to interfere and submerge the urge to react aggressively. This can be done with the help of NLP as it increases the speed of functioning of the unconscious mind. It trains the mind to have a say in important matters, recognize the conflict and teaches it to accept that conflict is nothing to fuss over.

When a difference in opinion arises in both parties, a middle ground can be reached through mutual compromise, or at the very least a mutual respect can be introduced. Thus, mountains will not be made out of molehills, and estrangement cases can be avoided. With the globalization of world, at some point or the other in life, many couples live in different countries in order to pursue their professional life. With this, infidelity has emerged to be a common issue as people move on quickly and leave behind old relations. NLP trains human nature to not give in to the temptation of a lucrative offer, be it emotional or physical. It raises our conscience so that we don't fall in to the trap of cheating on our partner.

Techniques used in Neuro Linguistics Programing

Presuppositions

Aside from the basic principle discussed ion the preceding section, NLP also uses other presuppositions that serve as foundations for its techniques. These presuppositions define NLP's understanding of the neurological, lingual and behavioral environment, both your own and other people's respective environment.

These presuppositions also provide additional insight on the core principles of NLP. Take note that these are a few of the many presuppositions of NLP, for every specific application of NLP in a particular field such as in a corporate or therapeutic setting, there will be corresponding presuppositions. Those listed below are some of the more general presuppositions that are applicable to a wide variety of fields. Some of these presuppositions are:

1. The map is not the territory. NLP believes that as human beings, we can never fully know or comprehend reality. Our understanding of the world around us is limited and can only be interpreted by our perception of reality. As humans, we can only rely on our senses to experience reality. This means that in NLP, it is this mental map not the actual physical territory itself that determines our behavior. Therefore, it is not reality itself that prevents or allows us from reaching our objectives or attaining success, but our individual perceptions.

2. All resources for success are within you. This is an important extension of the presupposition listed above. This means that since it is not the external reality but your internal perception of reality that can hinder or facilitate success; you already have the means to achieve success. Within each of us is a vast wealth of untapped potential that can create the success which all of us deserve. Only a few people, such as those successful people whom the founders have studied, have been able to tap into their potential for success. Through NLP, you can be guided in accessing your reservoir.

3. The need for respect for another person's perception. This means that since you have your own perception of reality, others too will have their own. Each person will have their unique perception, neither you nor other people have the correct, better or truer version of reality. Instead of challenging their perception, NLP recommends respect and empathy. You alone are responsible for your mind and your perception and you alone are accountable and privileged with the fruits of the efforts of your mind. The same goes for others, each of them are responsible and accountable for their own perception.

4. Understand through ecology not isolation. NLP advocates that every behavior cannot be understood in a vacuum. Our behavior, the thoughts behind them and the words we use are linked with each other. Each person is part of a sub-system, which is in turn part of a larger system. We cannot discuss one behavior, thought or word in isolation and contain its discussion with the person who has them. The interactions we make create an infinite network of permutations and combinations and it is impossible for a person to be unaffected by another.

5. People are not their behaviors. NLP encourages us to differentiate between the person and their behavior. A behavior may be reflective of the person's thoughts and words but the behavior is not the entire person. It is only a facet of the greater person as a whole. This is an important presupposition because through this concept, we can accept the person but correct the behavior.

6. The Law of Requisite Variety. This law states that the person who has the most flexibility in his behavior will have the most control over an environment. This means that to achieve your goal, you must have control over your situation. The more options you have, the more control you can exert. In NLP, it is encouraged for you to have a set of solutions to a particular problem or a set of steps towards a specific goal. This is because the world around us changes from time to time and if you have more than one option, solution or step, you can adjust and be flexible as the situation demands it. This way, if one solution you employ does not produce your intended result, choose another.

7. There is no failure only feedback. The ever changing sub-systems and systems in which we all belong are in a constant state of self-organization. Any changes introduced in the system will create ripples of change that aim to incorporate the change and restore balance once again. This means that when you fail at reaching solving your problem, it is not actually a failure but rather a feedback of the system that your solution is inappropriate.

Anchoring

Anchoring or self-anchoring involves establishing a connection be-tween an emotion and a stimulusi. Anchors refer to stimuli that arouse certain emotions and stimuli. For example, the smell of freshly baked bread arouses childhood memories. The smell of smoke arouses trau-matic experience. A touch can bring to mind comforting memories. A red traffic light elicits frustration. A blinking red light stimulates alert-ness. These anchors are often involuntary. The eExperience of these particular stimuli arouses thoughts, memories and emotions without the individual being aware of the trigger.

In NLP, a desirable emotional state is attached to a physical stimulus. A good illustration is the Pavlovian model of conditioning. A dog sali-vates when it sees food. The dog is "anchored" to another stimulus that elicits the same reaction (salivating). A bell rings every time food is given. Over time, the dog has anchored the thought food to the sound of a bell. The dog starts to salivate whenever it hears the bell ringing. Hence, the salivation is anchored to the ringing bell.

This same conditioning can be done in humans. A particular emotion is anchored to a physical stimulus. NLP harnesses the ability of an-chors in eliciting thoughts and feelings. It aims to anchor triggers iunto more positive and productive feelings and thoughts. Triggers can be conditioned to arouse happiness, confidence and improved energy. This technique allows a person to evoke positive and desirable feel-ings and thoughts when faced with negative emotions and situations. It is much like invoking positive emotions in demand.

How to set an anchor

To set an anchor, follow these steps:

1. Choose a memory
Pick a particular memory that elicits a strong emotion. For example, if one wants to anchor a feeling of confidence, think of a particular moment when one felt or experienced confidence. Feelings that have been experienced before are best better and more powerful than the ones that have not yet been experienced; although imagining the self in the desired state may also work, but with less effectiveness.

2. Association into the memory
This step involves reliving the memory. See the event replay itself in the mind's eye. Relive the moment vividly. Recall all the sensory information from the event- the sights, smells, sounds and feel of ev-erything in that particular moment. Intensify the feelings evoked by the memory. Clearer images evoke more intense feelings. This way, the anchor becomes stronger and more effective.

3. Anchoring

Once the desired positive feelings are evoked by the memory, it is time to start anchoring the feeling. Create a trigger when the feeling is evoked. Once the feeling of, say, confidence, is felt, start rubbing the thumb and forefinger together. Keep doing this physical act until the feeling reaches its peak.

4. Release

When the desired emotion is at its peak, release the trigger. That is, stop rubbing the fingers together.

5. Test the Anchoring

This is called breaking the state. Do another activity to temporarily take the mind off anchoring. Perform this unrelated activity for about 30 seconds. Then start to test the anchoring. Perform the trigger (rubbing the fingers together). See if the trigger sets off the desired feeling. You know it works if the invoked feeling is as strong as it did in memory.

6. Practice makes perfect

Keep repeating the anchoring technique to induce the desired feeling faster. Repeat anchoring at least 3 to 4 times. Also, it is recommended to try different memories that elicit the same desired positive emotion. This way, the positive outcome is intensified.

Different Forms of Anchoring

Anchors come in different forms. To the uninitiated, anchors often happen with the person unaware of the link between the trigger and the emotion.

Automatic and Unconscious Anchors

Sometimes, a person may be aware of the response, but does not understand what the triggers and anchors are. Most often, the responses are automatic that a person dismisses it as something totally unrelated. Often, people consider moods and emotions as something separate from the current state of mind and the present situation.

Designer Anchor

Designer anchors are consciously created anchors used by demand. The individual willfully produces anchors to invoke desired positive emotions that can be of help in a given situation.

Kinds of Anchors

Anchors are based on sensory triggers. It may be visual, auditory or kinesthetic.

Visual Anchor

Visual anchors are visual stimulations. These anchors may be external or internal. External visual anchors can be anything from a small bracelet or a ring. Make sure that this type of visual anchor is ready to use any time. It is more convenient if the chosen external anchor is something that can be worn. While looking at a breathtaking landscape helps in feeling calm and confident, it is something that cannot be carried around. While this will be an effective anchor, it is of very limited use.

An alternative would be to carry an internal image of the said landscape. This way, the image can be brought to mind any time the anchor is needed. Most visual anchors are of the internal type. These are images imprinted and stored in the mind and recalled at will to stimulate desired emotions. Most common internal visual anchors include:

• People

Faces of people influential to in the individual's life can be conjured at will and made as anchors. These people can be friends, families, mentors or even famous personalities that the individual looks up to or treats as an inspiration.

• Symbols

Images of different symbols brought to mind can be used as internal anchors. Example, the mental image of a circle can be used as an anchor to trigger relaxation and calmness. The peace symbol can be used to eliminate anger.

• Landscapes

Seeing the wonderful natural lights can be inspiring. However, these landscapes cannot be possibly toted around as visual anchors. What one can do is to commit the landscape to memory in vivid detail. Then use this imagery as an internal visual anchor.

• Events

Memorable events are memorable mainly because of the emotions they have created. Think of how it felt when one first received recognition for a job well done. The euphoria of that exemplary achievement can be used as an anchor when one needs to boost confidence and determination.

• Memorable objects

Some memorable objects may be inconvenient to bring along. Objects such as a teddy bear, a blanket or a trophy is not a good idea to bring along to, let's say, an interview. However, if these objects are powerful enough to trigger emotions, keep a mental image of them instead.

Auditory Anchor

Sounds can be powerful anchors, too. They can be external or internal. External auditory anchor is an outward sound like whistling. It is fairly common to hear people who whistle when they are afraid. Internal auditory anchors are sounds or voices that one recalls. One can use a "voice in the head" saying a repetitive phrase such as "Keep calm".

Kinesthetic Anchor

Touch can also be an anchor. As with the other two types, it can be external or internal. Actually touching the body is an external anchor. The fingers can be rubbed together, the earlobe can be touched or a circle can be created with by the thumb and the second finger; all these are examples of kinesthetic anchor. Internal would be the mental image of touching such as imagining a hug or a comforting pat on the shoulder.

Swish Pattern

Swish pattern involves the replacement of an undesirable emotion with a more desirable one. This technique is based on the foundation that every memory has an attached emotion. Emotions can be good, sometimes bad or undesirable. Using the Swish technique, an individual will use the desired feeling from a good memory and tag it into the bad memory in order to replace its undesirable effect.
To further illustrate, here's the step-by-step guide:

• Recall a good memory. Picture it in vivid detail, especially the feelings that this memory evokes.

• Concentrate on the desirable feeling that the good memory brought about and amplify it. Hold that feeling.

• Next, think of a bad memory. An undesirable feeling will start to surface with the bad memory.

• When the bad feeling starts to bubble in the surface, revert the mind to the good memory.

• The good feeling returns. Hold unto on to that feeling.

• Revert the thought back to the bad memory. By this time, the previous bad feeling will have waned. This is because the feeling form the good memory is starting to last longer and overlaps into the bad memory. This way, the good feeling is starting starts to last longer and nudges the bad feeling that reverting to the bad memory causes. Concentrate on the good feelings.

• Keep "swishing" back and forth between the good and bad memory until such time that the mind and the body sustains the good feelings longer.

So basically, the swish pattern is playing a good and bad memory back and forth, until the good feeling (from the good memory) nudges out the bad feeling (from the bad memory). The good feeling is then tagged into the bad memory so that the undesirable feeling is eventually removed. Whenever the bad feeling starts to surface when recalling a bad memory, the mind is shifted into the good memory.

For example, think of what excites you most. A trip to Europe. The first time you went on an exciting trip invokes a nervous feeling but the good kind. The kind that says "It's my first time, I don't know what to expect but I bet it's going to be a lot fun." Hold that good feeling. Then think about going up on stage to speak in front of hundreds of people. That thought alone could trigger anxiety- the bad kind.

Thinking of speaking in front of strangers will cause this kind of feeling- "I am nervous about this speaking thing. I don't know these people and I'm scared of what might happen." Now, when this negative feeling starts to surface, immediately revert to thinking about the trip you took and the excitement that came with it. The good feeling will return. Then swish back into the thought of speaking in front of strangers. The negative feeling will have some sort of a lag before you start feeling that undesirable anxiety.
Once the anxiety starts, revert back to thinking about the good memory of the trip. Keep swishing between the memories. The more you do this, the longer the residual effect of the good feeling becomes, until such time that the good feeling already encroaches into the thought of speaking in front of other people. By then, the undesirable feeling will be replaced by the good excited feeling. This way, the anxiety will be significantly decreased.

Framing and Reframing

Framing is considered as an emotional de-amplifier or amplifier. That is, it can intensify or weaken emotions, depending on what the individual needs. This NLP technique works by correcting or rebuilding the links in the limbic system, particularly between the hippocampus and the amygdala. This technique is very simple, yet very effective.

The framing technique used in NLP works based on the concept that memories are actually emotionless. Emotions and memories are totally separate from each other. To illustrate, the brain stores memories and emotions in totally different areas. Memories are stored in the hippocampus and emotions are processed by the amygdala.

Surprisingly, these two brain areas lie next to each other. What seemingly connects emotions to memories is the link that forms between the hippocampus and the amygdala. That is, when memories are stored, these this form a link with whatever emotions that happen to be present in the amygdala at that precise moment.

Framing seeks to rearrange that connection. It simply tries to cut the link between a memory and a bad emotion and reconnect that memory to a more useful and desirable emotion. In NLP, there is positive and negative framing. Positive framing is amplifying a normal memory into something strong and vivid. Negative framing is dulling a memory in order to suppress the undesirable emotions it invokes.

For example, a nice memory of someone important to you can be positively framed. It just means amplifying the memory, making it more detailed and vivid. The feelings that come from it will also intensify. You can also use the positively framed memory in other NLP techniques such as anchoring.

Reframing
Reframing means changing how one looks at a certain memory or situation. It simply means looking at it in a different perspective. Instead of dwelling on the negative aspect of a situation, reframing helps in looking at it in a more empowering manner.

For example, having a disastrous interview can cause all sorts of negative emotions. Instead of dwelling on the frustration and self-doubt, look at this situation in a different way. Think back on how the interview went and use it as a learning process. What went wrong? Think of the things that made the interview less than good. Identify them and make a note of how to avoid the same mistake in the future. Then look at what you could gain from the bad situation. That is, the job may not really be suited for you because your skills are aimed for something better.

Failing that interview means that you will have another shot at another job that may even turn out to be the better choice for you. Reframing is basically trying to see what good one can get out of a seemingly bad situation. It puts a bad situation in a different light in order to make better decisions.

Loop Break

The loop break NLP technique is consciously altering or stopping an unconscious process. It means being aware of the looping process that the body tends to automatically enter into and breaking the loop. This technique is highly effective when trying to control higher alpha brain activities or highly emotional states such as anger, fear, anxiety, stress and rage.

For example, a person loses his head when facing frustrating situations. Car breaking down on the way to work when you are already late for a very important meeting can easily cause you to blow your fuse. Frequent responses would be kicking the car, cursing and shouting.
A colleague or subordinate failing to turn in an important part of a client presentation, which could mean losing an important account. The natural reaction would be to shout and berate the colleague. Now, this action will not finish the report nor win the client. It will just result in more anger and hurt feelings. All these reactions do nothing to remedy the situation. It takes away energy that can otherwise be channeled into actually solving the problem.

During a highly emotional states such as those illustrated above, the amygdala, hippocampus and the rest of the body quickly form a loop reaction. The loop bypasses the frontal lobes that are responsible for behavior moderation and decision-making.
By using the loop break, you can stop the unproductive angry outbursts. You can also control your behavior more effectively. In simple terms, loop break is much like "closing the eyes, taking a deep breath and counting to ten before reacting to a situation". During that short span of time, you are actually giving the frontal lobes a chance to start functioning at moderating the behavior. To make it more effective, one can consciously force the frontal lobes to start up by having a prepared "comfort thought". It is more like having a good thought to block off the loop that a negative situation usually provokes.

Here is an illustration:

The day is not going well. The car won't start immediately. After you got the car going, you get stuck in traffic. A few blocks away from the office, someone hits the back of your car. Instead of getting into a traffic-related altercation, just get the license plate number and the driver's name and contact details. Make a mental note to deal with this later. Going into an argument would only make matters worse.
Besides, you are now very late. You have a client presentation in 30 minutes. You have worked days and nights oin your part of the presentation. A team member failed to do his part of the presentation. A bad presentation will lose this client, which is a major account for your company. Instead of losing your cool and shout at your colleague, think of how to remedy the situation. 30 minutes is not enough time; but still, time that can be used to remedy the situation. Rush off some last minute changes to make the client presentation less of a disaster.

In both situations, the loop of getting into angry outbursts is broken. The person consciously blocked off the natural desire to just lose it. Instead, the time and energy were channeled into something more positive, which helped towards solving the situation or at least alleviating it.

Meta Model

This is a therapeutic technique that is helpful in understanding the problems of other people and making them understand those problems better. The Meta Model "deconstructs what the other person is saying in order to uncover the underlying cause of the problem.

When problems arise, the subconscious mind actually knows the solution already. Most of the time, some people don't like the obvious solutions, hence, they continue to try finding to find what they perceive are better solutions.

Mirroring

Mirroring is the most commonly used NLP technique. It is simply mimicking the behaviors and gestures of the person you are speaking with. You can copy with subtlety one's speech patterns, their body language, their tempo, pace, tone, pitch, and the volume of their voice, and the specific words they normally repeat.

Is NLP the same as hypnosis?

Hypnosis is a "unique" state of mind wherein it is mindful, relaxed, and highly suggestible. When one is in a state of hypnosis, it is easier to control your brain.

To practice hypnosis, choose a comfortable armchair or bean bag. You are supposed to be in an inclined position. You need someone you can trust, to perform this with you. Hypnosis won't work if you don't trust your hypnotizer. Hypnosis uses positive terminologies to be more effective and it makes use of the power of persuasion to control the mind.

How difficult is it to Use NLP?

One of the reasons that NLP is gaining in popularity is that the techniques and tools can be mastered quickly, and without too much difficulty or effort exerted.

The processes associated with NLP are easy for nearly anyone to understand and start using right away. You do not need to read tons of material or take special classes and training seminars. The straightforward processes introduced in this book are all you need to get the controls reset for both your emotions and behavior. You can work on as many things as you wish.

As long as you have a few minutes to devote to NLP each day and keep a notebook handy you will make progress. It can be done at any time of the day or night, although you should try and set up a regular time so that you develop a good habit of daily NLP sessions. Make sure you keep progress notes so that you can give yourself a pat on the back as you progress towards the change you desire to make. You will see a change start within days and can be right where you want to be within weeks. It makes the reality of years of therapy an alternative path you will not want to take anymore.

Within this book, there are numerous techniques and tools that have been mentioned to help anyone master the art of using NLP. It is important to note that although NLP promises relatively quick results, it is not a quick fix type of therapy. In some cases, it requires basic repetitive practice, so as to get the techniques correct and, of course, so that one can enjoy the full benefits that NLP has to offer.

Chapter 3: General Principles of Neuro Linguistic Programming

There are some Fundamental Principles or Presuppositions in NLP that are meant to shape the outlook with which NLP is used. They enable the user to use NLP in the way it was designed to be used. NLP is not just a collection of disorganized techniques for 'doing things for others'. That is not what it was designed to do. People who are formally trained in NLP use it quite differently and are aware of the limits of it.

In this chapter, we shall study the working principles of NLP that have been around since NLP was invented. Internalizing them will help you use NLP in the best manner. These principles or presuppositions are not idealistic. In fact, they are pragmatic, and they provide clear guidelines on the way NLP is to be used. Not following these can lead to the detriment of other people quite easily. So make sure you remember these fundamental principles of NLP while practicing it.

General Principles
• NLP is not a theory but a model. And the study is subjective in nature. It is an experience that differs for everybody.

• Rather than seeing NLP as a repair model, one should see it as a generative model. This means that NLP doesn't focus on finding or analyzing the reasons/causes for a problem, rather it focuses on finding the solutions for the problems. The choices are added in NLP, not taken away.

• The mind and the body make up one system.

• Every aspect of human behavior can be attributed a structure.

• How you use your representational systems will affect your external behavior.

• If something can be done by one person, it can potentially be done by any person.

• The capacity of the conscious mind is very limited

Social Interaction
• You have to take responsibility for the response you get from others.

• Whether people currently realize this or not, you have to act as if they possess all the mental resources they need at any particular moment.

• To influence people, you have to first see the world in their own unique perspective. You must begin by discovering their perceptions of the world and meeting them there before you can start to influence them.

• People make the best decision in any situation with the resources they have or believe they have.

• You must realize that there is no single version of truth for everyone. Each person has a different view of reality, and it is different from yours doesn't make it any less true than yours. They are all just different versions of reality, like a map of a territory, which is different from the real territory.

• People will always react to their internal version of reality and not exactly what they feel with their senses only.

Personal Development
• The individual who possesses the greatest behavioral flexibility is at the biggest advantage. He or she can influence the outcome the most. So make sure you augment your behavioral and attitudinal elasticity.

• Tell yourself that every problem has a solution.

• You must understand the identity and self-image of a person by differentiating it from their behavior.

• Every behavior or act is positively intended, at least on some level, in any person's life.

• If what you are doing doesn't seem to work, take it as feedback and refine your approach constantly.

Note: An important thing to remember is that these principles are not hard truths or facts. Rather, in NLP, we take each truth to be a working hypothesis. There will be situations where the principles will not hold true, and that is alright. The key is to act as if the principles are always true. Some of them can seem far-fetched, but acting as if they are true pushes us to constantly change how we interact with others until we get our point across or accept that they are not receptive to it

Rapport

The foundations of NLP are called its four pillars: rapport, sensory acuity or awareness, outcome-based or outcomes thinking, and behavioral flexibility. These pillars constitute the basis of the NLP philosophy and they support all the NLP presuppositions. Emphasis on these pillars during communication is important in changing something about people's lives. Using these pillars, people can reduce or even eliminate instances of miscommunication and help increase mutual understanding. Each of the four pillars is discussed in one chapter starting with rapport.

The Gift of Rapport

People communicate with one another to build relationships. One of the most important benefits of the NLP approach to people is in relationship building. In today's society, practically all people are driving in the fast lane. Cognizant of the pace by which people live and work, one of NLP's foundations imparts an important lesson in saying "no" to requests or favors that will add an extra burden on a person's busy schedule but will be sincere or effective enough to ensure that friendship or professional relationships are retained. This is called rapport - knowing how to build relationships and if necessary, handling the part where one needs to break some relationships off.

NLP suggests that success can be achieved when an individual is able to forge positive relationships with other people through rapport. It is important to mention at this point that success in NLP is facilitated if one has good rapport with his own self. Look back to one of the presuppositions of NLP - the meaning of communication from one person to another is the reaction one gets regardless of the purpose of such communication". Restating this in a simpler form, the meaning of communication to the receiver is the response the giver gets. Based on this presupposition, when there is misunderstanding about or resistance to a specific communication, the likely reason is lack of rapport.

The goal of improving or creating rapport is never "wholesale" agreement to everything that is communicated. Rather, rapport should properly make the other person understand what is being communicated. Rapport helps people get the message across. When you say "blue", rapport should make it easy for another person to understand that you said "blue". Based on the foregoing discussion, rapport is defined as the ability to communicate meaningfully with another person or with a group of people based on mutual understanding, trust, and congruity.

Benefits of Rapport Building

The advantages of building rapport with significant people in your life and with people around you are summarized as the 5 Rs:

• Recall: It takes good rapport to get people to recall you easily. When people recall you, you have come across well the very first time you met this person or when you were first introduced.

• Recognition: A person with good rapport creates impact with people he/she meets. First impression lasts. Remember, you never get a second chance to make a first impression. Make you first meeting count.

• Reaction: It is always an exhilarating feeling to elicit a positive reaction from someone during your next encounter after meeting him/her for the first time.

• Respect: Good rapport offers you a chance of earning people's trust. When people trust you, you gained their respect. You earn respect in how you cooperate and assist people.

• Responsibility: While it is true that a good relationship can be created with either or both parties exhibiting good rapport, successful people make it their responsibility for building rapport with others. This is good practice in any relationship. The one who is active or more active in building or improving rapport is the one in control of the relationship.

Techniques in Building Rapport

Creating rapport is something one can learn and train to be good at using NLP. However, unlike chemistry or biology, where one can gain experience and hone expertise in the confines of a laboratory, rapport is mastered when you are immersed in society as you build ad nurture relationships with people you live and work with. The strategies in NLP consist of basic skills and more advanced techniques. Some of the most important approaches to build rapport with others are discussed below.

The key skills in building rapport are:

• Inquiring
• Listening
• Organizing, and
• Researching.

Develop a positive attitude of curiosity towards other people. Being interested in people exudes an air of concern. People usually get the message that you care and you give a damn when you show interest in them. Through research, using an observational approach, for example, try to work out the best strategy to approach a person if you have not been introduced formally. Whatever approach you use, you need to properly communicate your intention. Asking something relevant is a good way to break the ice. After your purposeful inquiry, listen attentively to the response(s) given.

Be alert and look for opportunities to create rapport. Offer assistance if you believe they need it. If you are applying rapport in NLP in the workplace or in business, relationships may be more about alliances rather than friendship. Rest assured, however, that NLP is applicable in all settings and fields of human interest.

Rapport involves being able to see-to-eye with other people and connecting with them on the same wavelength. The fact is: a big chunk of how other people perceives your sincerity when you communicate with them is NOT based on the words spoken, but rather, how you say it in terms of:

• Facial expression;
• Gesture(s);
• Posture;
• Tone of voice; etc.

Matching and Mirroring
Here is where the "neuro" part of NLP comes in. One of the most effective techniques for building rapport on the "neuro" end is through matching and mirroring. Experts suggest that matching and mirroring are ways by which a person can become highly attuned to how another person thinks and experiences the world. The traditional method of listening is hearing words using one's ears. In NLP, matching and mirroring allows a person to listen not just with the ears but with the whole body.

Interestingly, as a person develops rapport, simple mirroring happens naturally. However, one has to be aware that there is a fine line dividing moving in rhythm with someone as in NLP and plain mimicry. People will always know if you are making fun of them.

In the NLP approach, it is suggested that when one wants to build rapport with another person, the one attempting to create rapport needs to match the following:

• Body gestures and position;
• Breathing rates;
• Rhythm of movement and energy levels; and
• Tone of voice and talking speed.

Some Rapport Exercises

The following rapport exercises will help in enhancing your skill in this pillar of NLP:

Exercise No. 1:

Look for a person you do not know very well. Start a conversation with that person and practice mirroring his/her body position and movements. Do not get into trouble by getting caught. Make sure to wait about 5 seconds after the person made a movement before you mirror that position and posture. To ensure your safety in case you get into trouble, bring with you a copy of this eBook and explain the rapport exercise.

This is shooting two jet fighters with one missile: you get to practice mirroring and your communication skills aimed at rapport.

Exercise No. 2

Do this exercise after you have performed the above exercise a number of times and you are confident you have established rapport with your "unsuspecting" exercise partners. Look for a person you do not know very well, but this time, you are to assume that you and that person know each other and already have rapport. Your "map" in this exercise is that you have known this person for quite some time and you are supposed to naturally get along.

You may or may not succeed during your first try, but do this many times and you will learn the power of rapport. Never think of this activity as an exercise in manipulating people. If you succeed in this exercise, there is a very good chance you will successfully be able to change your life with NLP. If you can build rapport with other people, there is no reason why you can't build rapport with yourself. Use such self-rapport to empower you to be the change you want to be.

Sensory Acuity

How can one tell if he or she has the level of sensory acuity or awareness to support the life change being aimed for? Everyone has a sense of awareness of the environment. You can feel if someone you are talking to says he is fine, but he actually isn't. When you visit a friend's house you would have noticed how distinct the environment is, not just in terms of visible indicators like the color scheme and the skillfully designed interior and landscape, but also in terms of the scent and the sounds. Your sensory acuity is at work.

Sensory acuity or awareness is the second pillar of NLP. Sensory acuity is the ability to notice and differentiate among the different types of sensory information from the world around you. Of equal footing with man's ability to receive or notice such sensory evidence is the capability to understand and interpret what the senses tell you and use such understanding to come up with useful feedback or reaction. The sensory acuity that tides people over in this world is commonly under-developed yet. Can you imagine the immense power that can be available to all people if the acuity of their senses is further sharpened? Imagine no more because NLP can help enhance SA en route to the change people want in order to improve their lot.

Importance of Sensory Acuity

The primary importance of sensory acuity (SA) is that it is the foundation for the art of effective communication. Moreover, SA is significant in NLP for the following reasons:

• SA is needed to build rapport with yourself and other people;

• SA is a "must" for people who aim to inculcate changes in their life because SA helps them to read the "road signs" that will take them to their destination - CHANGE;

• SA bails people out of imminent failure or setbacks before they actually happen;

• With SA, people are in the best position to know if they are in the best state of excellence necessary to accomplish a goal or effect a change in their life.

An Exercise for Sensory Acuity

Please carefully read each step of the exercise and perform the required action before moving on to the next step. There are four steps. At the end of the activity, you would have realized how awareness of your surroundings can create positive and beneficial experiences for you.

1. Think of a situation at home or at work which, although far from being a serious matter causes you a certain degree of annoyance. Recall that event in your mind and imagine that instead of just a flashback of this situation in your thoughts, you are actually watching it on video. To help you concentrate, you may close your eyes. Watch this real-life film and listen to the soundtrack as it originally happened. Try to recall what you felt both physically and emotionally when this event

actually happened. (The author's irritating situation is being caught up in heavy traffic.)

2. Break state. This technique in NLP means you stand up, shake each of your arms and your legs. After the breaking state procedure, think of some music you are fond of, something that is completely opposite of the mood imparted by the real-life video's original sound-track. Chances are, your thoughts would lead you to a number of music pieces. Please choose just one. (The author had actually three pieces of music in mind: Highway Star by Deep Purple; Don't Stop Me Now by Queen; and Cars by Gary Numan. The chosen soundtrack was Highway Star).

3. Rewind your real-life video, and imagine you are in a film editing booth. Then, integrate the music soundtrack you selected in the second step. Do not replace the original sound, but just integrate your music like a movie theme. Watch the video with the added theme music.

4. Break state as in the second step. Run the video again, but this time delete the theme music you added in the third step. What did you notice about that real-life scenario?

When this author carried out this exercise in a seminar, watching the video during the third step did not evoke negative emotion as it did when the first flashback was run in the first step. However, the revelation in the exercise is that during the fourth step when the video was run again with the soundtrack deleted, there was no negative emotion felt. According to a professional who moderated the NLP seminar, most reactions to these exercises reported complete absence of neg-ative emotion during the fourth step. There were some who reported that the negative feeling was greatly reduced. This is the expected reaction or feedback to the exercise.

Honestly, there were a handful who reported no change in emotion during the first and fourth steps. Remember - in NLP, there are no fail-ures, only feedback. This particular reaction indicates a lower level of sensory acuity than most people who carried out the exercise. Prac-tice and training, particularly through NLP, significantly improve one's level of sensory acuity.

In this exercise, concrete evidence is established that sensory infor-mation can shape one's feelings. Learning to control or program (in NLP terms) your perception of the world can help you think positively and change your life for the better. This author used to bring a CD of Highway Star in the car to play in case of another annoying traffic situ-ation. Lately, however, after this author's sensory acuity has ultimately leveled up (thanks to NLP!), all that needs to be done is mentally recall the music without actually needing to hear it. This should bring to the fore another NLP presupposition that the body and the mind are intertwined.

Outcome Thinking

Outcome thinking refers to the practice of focusing one's mental energy on the change aimed at life instead of getting stuck on the problematic scenario that had to be changed. As a pillar of NLP, outcomes thinking seeks a balanced position that will lead to a win-win situation to reach an intended goal - a change in your life. A person's awareness of the subtleties of thinking can transform his abilities to direct his actions toward the goal - change. Your thinking influences the outcome of your efforts.

Outcome-based thinking is a process of systematically polishing and attuning goals or targets in order to achieve one's desired outcomes. The process of outcomes thinking reinforces the chances of attaining the desired change because when one focuses on refining his own plans and strategies to create an intended outcome, the mind is "programmed" to believe that the whole system is capable of doing it and the outcome can be realized.

A Training Exercise in Outcomes Thinking: Drawing Well-Formed Outcomes

There are a number of frameworks used to conceptualize well-formed outcomes. This framework was based on Peter McNab as enunciated in 2005. Think of something you want to change in your life as an outcome of this exercise. Carry this out seriously because this is the start of your journey of discovering something new for your life. Note the questions down in a diary or a notebook and answer them.

• What do you want to change in your life? State your answer in a positive tone. You should have at least partial control of this outcome.

• Where, when, and with whom do you want this change in your life to take place?

• What are the indicators that you have attained the desired outcome?

• Does your current behavior support the outcome or change you desire? If this behavior is not supportive of your goals, what will you lose if you change this behavior?

• Will the outcome you desire affect other areas of your life?

• In what particular areas or what particular circumstances will stop you from pushing for your desired outcome?

• What barriers, if any, do you perceive that prevents you from enjoying the outcome you desire at the present time? Do you need any additional resources?

• How do you plan to attain the outcome you want? When are you going to put your plan into action to get that outcome?

The answers you provide the questions, except the outcome itself, may need to be evaluated from time to time. You need to refine your answers to these questions and revise them accordingly to increase the probability to attaining your desired outcome. The above exercise constitutes the procedure in generating a well-formed outcome, which is the centerpiece or main focus of outcomes thinking. People should direct their efforts, particularly rapport, sensory acuity, and behavior flexibility, to reach the outcome they earnestly long for.

Flexibility

Behavioral flexibility, or flexibility in general, is the fourth pillar of NLP. The basic idea behind behavior flexibility is leading oneself towards the discovery of doing something different when the current behavior is not working to attain a desired outcome. Success in the practice of NLP is a matter of being flexible enough to do things which will facilitate the attainment of an expected outcome. Flexibility is important in the NLP approach to change one's life because ability to adapt one's actions to influence a particular response from another person, or in one's own self is a "must" to make the intended change a reality.

Behavior flexibility is a matter of habit. If habits can be broken, habits can also be made. Developing behavioral flexibility can be achieved through training and practice. One of the creators of NLP, John Grinder, suggested that each night, a person should reflect on the occurrences of the day as it ends and formulate at least three different ways of responding or reacting to the situation. This book extends Grinder's recommendation as follows:

• Write down in a diary, journal, or notebook specific situations that happened for each day. An electronic file-keeping system is best to facilitate classification and search.

• Categorize these situations into those which turned out positive and negative outcomes.

• Write down the response you made for the situations and classify those that worked and those that did not.

• Formulate at least three alternative responses for each situation and commit these alternatives to memory.

• Your responses to situations with positive outcomes may be repeated to verify if they work at all times or most of the time.

• Learn from the feedback you made about negative situations. The next time this negative outcome occurs in a similar case, try one of the alternatives you prepared as a response or reaction.

• After one month, organize your file and review your information. Adapt behaviors that consistently worked well for similar situations. You will be surprised how behavioral flexibility can make you a better person and your life a happier one.

Chapter 4: The Importance of Control

Control is a controversial topic, with different people approaching it in a myriad of ways. For most people, it requires being able to manage their lives and their surroundings. When a person feels as though they are in control of a situation, then they become less likely to experience emotions like fear and panic.

A short trip through the shows on television, these days show just how out of control many people feel and are when it comes to behavioral and emotional issues. There are entire reality shows devoted to people with chemical and alcohol addictions, serial cheating, hoarding and all manners of behavior issues. There are also movies that try to take on serious emotional control issues with humor, such as "Anger Management" starring Adam Sandler. Clearly there is an imbalance in society, and a need for reconciliation as so many people are out of control and they do not know how to handle this state of affairs.

The problem is these issues are the cause of a lot of misery for millions of millions of people. When a person is not in full control of their life, it can lead to divorce, depression and even suicide. It is nearly impossible always to be in control at all times, but even an 80% rate of emotional and behavioral control would seem like heaven to someone that is experiencing a severe lack in that particular department.

How Loss of Emotional and Behavioral Control Impacts Your Life

There is no greater feeling than that of being organized and in complete control of everything that is happening in your life. This allows one to live peacefully, and be able to breathe a sigh of relief when faced with particular challenges. However, life is not as simple as this, and there are many instances where one can lose control.

Not being able to control spending can lead to bankruptcy and divorce. Not being able to dial down the anger can lead to arguments or fights and legal problems. Chemical addictions can lead to job loss and health problems. Not being in control can have a lot of bad effects that drag your life down in ways you could never imagine until it is too late.

There is no doubt that not having adequate control over your emotions and behavior can make life difficult for you and those around you. Nervous and anxious individuals not only increase stress in themselves, but it ramps up the atmosphere of stress for anyone around. It is easy to tell yourself to "not worry" about things, but putting that into practice is not always easy. In fact, it is never easy if you have made a lifelong habit out of worrying about anything and everything imaginable. Gaining control should be placed as a priority in your life.

The issue in gaining control is the "how" to do so. The reason why things seem to fall apart is because one may have tried a number of times, but the correct tools and techniques are not being used. This in turn leads to a frustrating round and round process, whereby, a person keeps repeating the same action over and over, yet they are expecting the same result.
Gaining control is therefore all about modifying behavior, in such a way that one can see a marked difference in present circumstances.

Chapter 5: How Neuro-Linguistic Programming Is Used

"The only thing you sometimes have control over is perspective. You don't have control over your situation, but you have a choice as to how you view it."

Chris Pine

You can see from the above statement that in order to widen your perspective, you need to open up your mind to the perspective of others. Yes, you control what you perceive as being correct, though "correct" is objective and what other people see as "correct" will be different. By opening up how you view a given situation, you effectively give yourself more potential to find answers from every perspective, rather than narrowing those answers down to your own perspective.

Traditional therapy used in a situation when someone had problems examines the problems. However, Neuro Linguistic Programming doesn't do that. It simply looks for better outcomes. It doesn't spend time examining why you think in the way that you do, based on past experience. It simply teaches you to see answers from a wider perspective.

Perhaps the problem with traditional ways of looking at problems is that they create more problems and a patient would, for example, be made to go back through past events, which are negative anyway and expand upon their reasons why these events were so bad. All of this is a negative approach. This negativity may hold back potential.

One of the best things about this approach is that anyone of learning age can employ it. There is much scope for improving the outlook of, for example, a sales team. Instead of looking at the smaller picture of expected results, the team is taught to see the situation from all perspectives, including understanding the client's needs, wants and fears. With this knowledge the staff is able to sell more effectively to meet those needs and will be able to target specific markets successfully, rather than going into sales situations half blinded by old sales techniques, which don't work anymore.

The thing is that times are changing and people need to embrace the multi-cultural viewpoint as well as seeing the vast scale every situation presents. Neuro-Linguistic programming techniques allow them to do that. Thus, those learning these skills are more likely to succeed in a working environment.

This philosophical approach of Neuro Linguistic programming comes from a set of rules, which dictate how people react in given circumstances:

1. People don't outwardly try to fail. In fact, they do the best they can within the limited resources of their knowledge.

2. People can control the outcome of their lives because it only the individual who is in control of the thoughts that individual experiences.

3. You can't judge a person by what they do.

4. Everyone has the ability to succeed.

5. There really is no such thing as a failure. These should be thought of as reactions to a given stimulusi.

By looking at the above, the philosophy clearly puts the control of each person's destiny into their own hands. You can achieve what you want to achieve. You should not judge others and you should never see the word "failure" as part of your vocabulary. In fact, failure can be seen as reaction which is very helpful and could be thought of as feedback.

A typical example of this is when a child fails to grasp a mathematical equation. It's simply the point of view that cannot get in sync with the manner in which he is being taught. The child gets frustrated and learns nothing. The negative impact of this is that the child will hate math. However, using Neuro-Linguistic Programming approach, the problem can be explained at a level the child understands. The result would be that he would gain a positive experience. The failure in this case could be perceived to be that of the teaching methods. If a teacher employs Neuro Linguistic Programming techniques and shows the child a piece of cake and asks the child to share this between four friends, the child can see the task as simple, will cut the cake in half and then in half again and will have achieved an understanding of fractions, which can then be explained by the teacher. What the teacher gained is the child's perspective and used this to help the child's understanding. What the child gained was knowledge put in a way that he was able to understand. The end result was a very positive one, based on the teacher taking note of the child's original reaction to traditional teaching methods.

As you can see from this simple demonstration, the enrichment of the teacher's ability came from his open minded approach and that's what Neuro Linguistic Programming is all about. It may sound simple, but it does need to be learned in the classroom with qualified teachers because the subject is not all as simple to understand. These teachers have been shown ways, which have been proven to work with students and their experience in this field is what helps the student employ the techniques more effectively.

All things are possible and even plausible once you learn the principles of Neuro Linguistic Programming approach and the number of people who have benefited from this approach is growing all the time. Little did the people who came up with the philosophy realize the impact that this system of thought would have on all sectors in life. It is a system which has been proven to work and to enhance people's lives.

Embracing the fact that your knowledge may be limited, use this as a reason why you believe that Neuro Linguistic Programming approach can help to widen your perspective and help you to see the possibilities that lie ahead of you, instead of narrowing the range of those possibilities to any specific aims or goals. The goals in themselves limit the possibilities since these are self-contained and that is limited in itself. The wider picture always gives those who learn these techniques the edge over those that don't, but they also teach practitioners to use empathy toward others regardless of their level of understanding. It is this empathy that enriches relationships with others and helps to cement positive environments which are conducive to productivity, usefulness and the potential of reward. These rewards may not be financial, if NLP is used to help in the struggle with relationships, although it has monetary value for business people because people will enjoy doing business with someone who has learned the techniques.

The techniques are used to help open up levels of understanding that enable people to find solutions to problems, albeit personal or in their professional capacities. It's a system that is used successfully by people all over the world and the system has been put into different languages so that all can gain from the experience of learning a new way of thinking.

Chapter 6: Who Can Benefit From Neuro-Linguistic Programming?

"True learning involves learning other ways of doing what you can do already."

John Seymour

If you look at the above statement made by John Seymour in his book "Neuro Linguistic Programming: The New Psychology of Personal Excellence, you will see that anyone can benefit from using this system of by opening up the mind to possibility. Those who stagnate in the belief that they are doing things one specific way and that's the right way to limit their possibilities. They are simply telling themselves that they know how to do something the correct way and thus do not try to learn any other way because they see no need to.

If you use the same premise for all things in life, you could consider that an adult will have learned set ways to do most of the things that he does every day. Thus he closes off his mind to learning because he sees no need to improve upon what he already knows.

If you look at Neuro Linguistic Programming techniques, these involve opening up the mind to more ways to do a set task because your perspective is not the only one that exists. It may be to you, but universally, there's a whole new area of learning for you to embrace and try. If you hold yourself back on the premise that you already know everything, you stem your own personal growth.

Thus, looked at in this way, you can see that anyone can benefit from the use of Neuro Linguistic Programming. Widening the horizons of learning is always going to be beneficial at any stage in life. For example, someone may recognize the behavior of someone who they admire. They may wish to emulate that behavior, and to a certain extent, this is widening the scope of what they are currently able to do, and thus employs Neuro Linguistic methods. Others may not be able to communicate effectively and may use the system to help them to present their point of view in a much more logical and acceptable manner, which will get the point across.

People use Neuro Linguistic Programming for all kinds of things. For example, are you afraid to go on an airplane? Afraid of spiders? Well, Neuro Linguistic Programming may be helpful in teaching you to overcome those phobias, which are weighing down your life and making it miserable.

Another way to look at this is to examine the faces of people on a train in the morning. Each of these people will have created a personal "bubble" or protective shield against other passengers because that's how they protect themselves from harm. We all do it. Once you drop that shield, you actually open up understanding and are able to reach a higher potential because you are not locking yourself off from possibilities.

Using the techniques to better your life

People who are reading this book may be asking what good this is to them. Here's a demonstration of what the power of Neuro-linguistic Programming has for the individual. During your everyday life, something will annoy you or cause you to lose your temper. How you react says a lot about who you are and about how that anger makes you feel. There are several ways to react to a situation which makes you feel anger, as follows:

1. Be angry

2. Be understanding and empathetic

3. Remain inwardly angry

Looking at these three possibilities, you may think that the healthy response is to be angry. People say "get it out of your system" but in fact, when you are angry, you don't get it out. What you are doing is giving your inner thoughts problems. Anger provokes all kinds of negative reactions, such as regret, more anger, frustration and bleak thoughts. So anger achieves nothing that is positive. You may argue that if shouting makes you feel better, then it's positive, but is this kind of behavior really going to make you feel the better long term? You limit yourself by showing anger. The second option is the way the Neuro Linguistic Programming would teach you to understand. When you are understanding understand and empathizeetic, you don't feel any of the negativity that you would if you had displayed anger. Your mind is tranquil and you are able to move on from a bad situation much more quickly. If you take the third option and this may even come as a result to of taking the first option, then you prolong the angry feeling and thus limit your potential to move on from it.

Similarly, you can use Neuro Linguistic Programming to achieve what you want to achieve. The systems that you are taught are things such as detachment. This is where you take a situation which cause you negative reactions and you imagine it from a more neutral stance. For example, look on the situation as if it's happening to someone else instead of you. Play back the situation from the moment of negativity to what lead up to it, and you begin to see it differently and are able to then use this information to take away fears. You may have to do a rerun of the situation several times to see the pointers which are there to be seen.

This examining of situations is used to further your understanding, but imagine this. You watch the situation in your mind's eye. You see what lead up to the bad situation or fear and then rerun it again, but this time associate something hilarious with the images that you are looking at. It could be a funny song or something of that nature, but you then associate that music with that situation and are able to adjust your mind to seeing it differently, thus being able to take away the fear.

These are tools which can be used by anyone in any given situation and help them to see different ways to approach difficulties in life. There are many such tools employed in the use of Neuro Linguistic Programming and if this actually does seem an interesting subject to you, it would be worthwhile studying further with trained lecturers because they can show all of the techniques used and you can then apply them to your life

Begin before you begin, wrap up before you wrap up
This is like using hypnotherapy without other people noticing. If you handle sales people and you want them to rake in more sales, you can use this technique during one of your training courses or coaching sessions or even during a sales call with prospective buyers.

After the mandatory introductions, you can say a statement along these lines, "There are some things that I want to discuss before we begin..."

And then you start with the session! Some people often build walls every time they are subjected to a training session and the beginning is always the hardest. Before starting formally, you can tell them or your client that you expect to have a grand time as you work with them. You will never actually notice that you have actually started when the "real" session began.

On the other hand, if you have come to the conclusion of a sales pitch or training your sales agent, you can also finish before you can even make a "formal closing remark". You can simply say, "I guess that's all for the day," then get up and leave.

You may also say, "Oh, there's something I forgot..." and then begin again. Prepare to be amazed at what can transpire and how many sales you can make before you wrap up.

Take Other People Literally

Take them at face value. Take the things they say as they are. Ever wondered why most people cannot lose weight? It's because when you ask them what they want, they would tell you, "I want to lose weight." Taking that literally, the individual wants to lose weight. That person knows that they want to lose weight but ask them again why and you'll get an answer that they aren't sure how and they cannot picture themselves being slim.

Truth is, people don't like losing things; it'sit's how people are. So ask again, "What happens if you are slim?" Notice how the other person would light up because they can easily see a mental image of them being thin.

Using the same example, if you want to achieve your ideal weight, imagine yourself already thin and doing the things that you want to do.

Be There First

If you don't know where you're going, the journey would be a struggle. You have the power to change your mind. If you want to achieve success, you have to be able to go transition from your current set of circumstances to your desired set of circumstances.

When you want to influence others to achieve the things you have achieved, you have to "infect" them with your positive attitudes. When you go on meditation, you go into a state of calmness, love, happiness, and gratitude. You apply the NLP anchor technique here. Associate success with a happy event and stick to it until you are already in that state.

Being at your destination first is visualization – it helps you "transport" yourself even before you do it.

Gestures are Powerful

Gestures, mannerisms, and other non-verbal forms of communication are powerful. They can say a million different things. You can build rapport with another person by mirroring their gestures. It is the best way to build a good relationship. If you are into sales, you can use this to generate more sales and improve your productivity.

Milton Model

The Milton Model is named after a renowned hypnotist, Milton Erickson. He used the power of verbal hypnosis to generate the results he wanted. He used words that are "artfully vague". For instance, rather than saying, "Your body feels relaxed", he says, "You are beginning to notice sensations in your body," and you will start to notice the changes in your body.

You can look at it this way. You are now reading this book because there are things that you want to learn, and you are interested in discovering how you can apply the principles you have learned into practice.

If you read the above statements again, they may sound specific but they aren't. The words merely suggested what you will experience but they are always true for almost anyone.

This technique would help increase your productivity and output.

The Meta Model

The Meta Model is based on the theory that people do not experience direct reality, but they instead experience it through "maps" of reality that they themselves created in their minds. Whenever they are faced with adversity, it does not exist in reality but in the "map" of reality.

You have the power to change your "map" so that you can easily overcome the challenges. You enrich your reality "map" by the power of framing technique and/or the self-anchoring technique. Practice mind control and you change the course of your "map" of reality.

Do Not Hesitate

It is natural for people to hesitate when they find themselves in a situation where they have to decide on something.

Do this exercise. Identify the areas in your life where you are likely to hesitate. Decide that you would like to just go for it now. Choose a business establishment, like a store, shop, or restaurant, and make an absurd request, like ordering something that they do not sell. Keep a straight face, be polite, and do not threaten. Do this twice in a week. Think about the times when you have hesitated in the past and enjoy new responses today.

Why it will work

Your central nervous system is set up to protect you from dangerous situations. From childhood, people are taught to avoid making mistakes. But the truth is making mistakes is important for your growth and learning. The above exercise will help reduce hesitation and boost your confidence level. There are instances where hesitation is important, especially if you will be put in danger, like when crossing a busy street. Keep that in mind.

Chapter 7: The Power of Believing

There is a wealth of power behind words, and the meaning that they can attach to a person, situation or even a memory. How we perceive words will directly affect the way that we behave in a range of different circumstances.

How often have you had bad behaviors passed off as "habit?" Learned behavior can have a lot to do with how we pattern behaviors. Emotions can play a significant part in leading you to exhibiting some unwanted behavior. Young children learn early how to get their way in many situations. It is through crying or other peace disturbing behaviors like tantrums. Parents often relent in order to restore the balance of emotions in the home, car or grocery store.

Looking at emotions through the eyes of a child makes it easier to understand how powerful they are. This is simply because a child has not yet learned how to lie, and, therefore, has not tried to figure out how to hide the truth.
Therefore, when the young child is screaming, it can be said that they are doing so because they believe that they will be attended to by their parent or caregiver.

It takes years to learn effectively how to effectively assuage the emotions that send one into a spiral of immediate want of resolution or result. A lot of people never really master this skill. They get caught up in feeling the way they think and acting to reflect their thoughts is inevitable. This lets anyone off the hook when it comes to making the changes needed to improve emotional and behavioral control.

To make long lasting positive changes, it demands that you get an understanding of the basics that cause bad behaviors and loss of emotional control. It may seem like a bit of work at first, but you will soon start to recognize when the emotions are driving, and you can take the steps necessary to regain control.

Importance of Beliefs
One of the worst things that can be done is to put off bad behavior or complete emotional meltdowns as children are to have them passed off as "that is just how they are." It teaches people from the beginning that bad behavior is acceptable from you in certain situations simply because that is how you choose to handle things. It makes an individual weak from the start. It ends up making people search for the answers in the environment when it should be sought inside.

If it is indoctrinated in you that you will respond with external stimulus in such a way it is a belief. Having enough bad beliefs will guarantee that change will never occur. The beliefs we hold about anything and everything are what drive the subconscious mind. It is what determines what you will do, say and try to achieve consciously. It can be a goal oriented help or a barrier to ever gaining controls over the bad behaviors you want to correct. It can also leave you stranded on an emotional roller coaster your entire life.

If you believe that you will always get upset when someone tells you "no" you WILL always get upset when someone tells you "no." It may not be the kind of upset that is seen as a full blown tantrum, but you will have a hard time dealing with negatives and feel stress and anxiety. No matter how much you outgrow some behaviors and feelings they can stick with you for a lifetime if you do not understand them and strive to change them.

How Beliefs Are Made
Some of your beliefs are formed for you. It can be family or friends that tell you things about how you react to things, or even about your abilities. If they are good beliefs, it is a positive thing. More than likely it is where we gain out a lot of our bad beliefs. It explains away bursts of anger, impatience or even addictions to substances that harm your health. How easy is it for a smoker to quit if they are always told they can never quit?

Other beliefs emerge from experiences in life. If you are consistently bypassed for promotions and pay raises, you will eventually belief that you do not deserve them. You may experience numerous failed relationships and develop the belief that you do not make a good partner. If you believe negative ideals you will be stuck in that rut forever. This is why a lot of "talk therapies" take years to work, if they ever do. Until you make the realization that what you believe about yourself is what will determine your outcome you will never see real change.

The benefit of using NLP is that beliefs can be changed. This can be done quickly, and you will see results right away. This is great because someone can get so trapped in a bad belief, that it cripples them completely as they try to move towards their future. What may have taken years to get done in the traditional behavioral modification can be done in days or weeks. There is no magic to it. It is simply a matter of knowing WHY you do what you do and changing it.

In dealing with the why you do something the way you do it, you also need to address any core reasons, rather than situational factors. By understanding the root of the core beliefs, it becomes easier to make changes where necessary.

How to Change a Belief

You need to take some time and discover what your beliefs are when it comes to emotional control and behaviors. Take a notebook and start listing any and all of them you can think of. You may be surprised at what is lurking in your subconscious mind!

Quite a few beliefs really have no bearing on how you behave or emotionally react to things, but ones that do are called limiting beliefs. These are the ones you want to isolate and change for the better.

Here are a few examples of some limiting beliefs:

• I am always cranky in the morning.

• Being told no makes me mad.

• I've been drinking alcohol too long to quit now.

• I have no patience on the freeway.

• I am too old to get things done.

• You will want to change these to more positive beliefs such as:

• I look forward to a brand new day.

• Being told no makes me look at different opportunities.

• I can quit drinking alcohol because I am tired of it.

• Heavy traffic helps me work on defensive driving skills.

• Age has made me wiser and getters able to accomplish my goals. Actually switching them out is not as hard as it may seem. The action of changing a negative thought into a positive thought is an excellent NLP technique. Here is another simple process to do just that:

• Find a quiet location and close your eyes.

• Create a visual representation in your mind of the bad belief. (such as a fanged wolf or bat)

• Starting from a small little picture, grow this image really large in your mind.

• Gradually shrink it in your head until it virtually disappears.

• Using your arm (in your imagination) brush the tiny image of it away.

• Create a warm and positive image of the new belief you want to have.

• Grow it larger and larger until it fills up the mental screen.

• Open your eyes. You are finished!

• Repeat this daily until you start feeling different from that particular belief.

Placing Proper Value on Beliefs

To fully engage in any new belief that you install you need to give it a lot of values. It has to be the one thing you really desire to see change. This is a huge way that the 1% top money earners are able to focus so hard on creating wealth. They keep earning and amassing great wealth a lot of value. It becomes a sort of center in their personal universe. If you truly want to get anger or anxiety under control, the positive change needs to hold a great deal of value ftor you.

You can create the path that you need to take to be free of any undesired behavior or emotional turmoil. You can finally take the reins and control your life. The great thing is you can revisit this exercise and do it as often as you need to. You will find limiting beliefs that surface from time to time and you can tackle them as they become known to you. It is one of the most flexible and guaranteed ways to see real change quickly.

Become Liked by Everyone

When it comes to being everybody's trusted ally, or even becoming more efficient when it comes to persuading clients or selling a product or an idea, not everyone is on the same level. You would notice that some people behave differently, and some even look more appealing than others. It is not because they graduated on top of their class, or they are much more beautiful-looking than you. They simply have a certain effect on other people around them.

The good news is that learning how to control your body and the rest of your actions can help you in building a better communication and relationships with other people. That is also something that you can do with certain NLP techniques. Another good news is that rapport building and persuasion techniques of NLP is commonly taught, and knowing how they work with the everyday things you do would give you leverage.

Conforming Behavior Destroys Barriers

Animals and humans act similarly when it comes to trust – both tend to like creatures that are like them. You would probably have noticed that at school or at work – the teachers or bosses who would often do you favors are those who believe that they are somewhat like you. A parent is also bound to have a favorite among his children when he sees that one of them takes after his positive traits.

When you are trying to build rapport, you are technically not forcing someone to look at the world your way – you will find that what you are trying to do is to make the other person think that you are thinking the same way. That means that if you present him a certain solution to a problem, you are making it look like that a person like you, who is very similar to him, has come up with an answer. So, that answer is more likely to appeal to him. That means that somehow, there is truth in the saying "if you can't beat them, join them."

Here is a common rapport-building NLP technique, called matching behavior. It means that when you match the physical and linguistic behavior of another person, you are more likely to break his barriers that he tends to build between himself and another person. Here is an example:

Person A goes inside an audio store, wanting to buy headphones. Person A says to Person B, who is the salesman, that he likes how the headphones LOOKS on the stand, but he doesn't want the exact item because it SEEMS suspicious and he doubts if that stock still works properly. Person B, however, doesn't have any other similar item in the stockroom, and he wants to get the sale. Person B says "I will take a LOOK," and checks if the item is still working properly. He comes back, and tells his customer that "the headphones APPEARS fine to me." Person B gets the sale.

With that example, you would notice that the customer pays attention to the world, using his sense of sight mainly. That is the case even if he is trying to buy a gear that he would use with his ears! Now, Person B knows that he would get the sale if he makes it a point that he is on the same page as the other person, meaning they share the same perspective when it comes to judging products.
The same technique is being used by police interrogators and psychologists to establish connection and trust, then to extract information. That means that when people use the same language, they are more likely to get along!

Radiate Positivity

Do you ever wonder why charming people would continue to be charming, no matter what they look like? You have probably seen people who are shorter or fatter than you, but it seems that they have more friends than you do. You have seen people who lack limbs, but it seems that they have more athletic friends than you would ever have been in this lifetime. Don't you ever feel envious?

Here is what these people do to others – they make it a point that they feel and act unstoppable, and that is the reason why they know they have a much bigger life than everyone else. The reason is that you are going to attract people that are similar to you. Now, if you think that you are ugly, incompetent, and a big failure, you might begin being scared of what kinds of people you are attracting.

If you want to gain more friends and be a positive influence to other people, just become that person you want to be. Instead of being frustrated at the world, smile and keep performing at the top. Sooner or later, people will pick up and follow your lead. You will be happy that you behaved that way. You may not realize that now, but you will understand that later on.

Everybody Focuses on Themselves

If you want to build instant rapport every time you are introduced to someone, you do not have to sell yourself most of the time. That means that if you have previously felt anxious when meeting other people, you can always think that other people generally put their own interests over you. When you think about that, you do not have to feel conscious about being placed ion a spotlight when you need to talk to someone you do not know. Instead, put the spotlight on them!
You do not have to be afraid that you are under scrutiny when you need to talk to people – more often than not, they are thinking and paying more attention to how they behave or how they make an impression on you. Also keep in mind that people are also receptive and responsive to their environment – calm down and talk the way you want them to respond to you. Use that line of thinking to your advantage – make a subtle mirroring of their actions, and then give them a subtle compliment. That feeds their need for validation, and they would soon remove the barriers that make the conversation uneasy for both of you. With you acknowledging the good in them, they would be more likely to give you more information about themselves.

Chapter 8: The Basics of Total Emotional Control

How much easier could your life be if you could manage your emotions in an instant? How much better would you get along with co-workers, supervisors, family members and friends if you could be in complete control of your emotions? It is often emotional instability that leads to bad behaviors. A good example is that it takes feeling anger before you yell or pick up and throw things, right?

Many people strive to achieve balanced emotions, by increasing their awareness in regards to how they behave and how the react in certain situations. Although it would be excellent to say that people always behave well, a large amount of what is remembers remembered is the negative or bad behavior. These are the emotions that drive people to doing the worst out of control things.

Recognizing the rise of uncontrolled emotions is where the key lies in derailing bad behaviors. Imagine how ground breaking this can be if you suffer from chronic bouts of depression, or have difficulties in dealing with workplace bullies and gossips. It does not replace the need for professional counseling, or taking medications in some instances. What it WILL do is give you an edge in changing a bad mood to a good one. It will help you curtail emotions that can overwhelm you in an instant and make you nonproductive.

This does not mean that you are pushing emotions down or not feeling anything. You will still experience every type of emotion, but in a more controlled and uniform way. You will not be led by emotions, which is critical to feeling that life is stable and obstacles can be managed. You can finally view a disappointment as something less than life-altering and a statement of your overall abilities to achieve anything. It brings a healthy balance.

When you being makinghave made NLP a part of your daily life, you will learn more and more how you can control your emotions by thinking positively. This basically entails flipping the switch on all negative thoughts that come your way. To begin, this is something that you will be doing consciously. However, as time goes on, you will find that you are able to control your emotions subconsciously.

The Body-Mind Link

There is the volume after volume written on the skill and abilities of our mind to pick up on body language. Much of human communication is done without ever speaking or reading a single word. The mind is trained from early stages to read physical cues as to how someone is feeling or how receptive they are to talking with you. The amazing thing is that the mind can do this with your body. It picks up on the standard cues you give it to create the mood you are in currently.

The benefit of knowing this is that it gives you all of the proof you need to understand that you can control your moods far more than you ever thought possible. The way you sit, stand, breathe and view everything will ultimately cue your body to take on a mood. The next time you are feeling an extreme emotion of sadness or anger take note of all the physical cues you are giving your body. Each is unique to an individual, but most people that are depressed or sad will slouch and breathe slow.

Think of the extremes of any situation. How do you carry yourself if you are angry? Do you breathe harder and heavier? How about when you are really happy or excited? Changing the cues you give to your brain can instantly change your mood. This does not mean that you will feel instantly happy about losing a job or getting an eviction notice, but it does mean that you do not have to stay in depressed and dark place.

Your body language, or nonverbal communication, is also a key way that you can pass on a method. Using NLP means that you are more aware of how your body works together with your words to ensure that your message goes across clearly and authentically.
Take for example, you are delivering an informative lecture on a geographical subject. To emphasize on certain points, you may use your arms to make shapes that will help describe the features that you are talking about. Slow movements, such as simple pacing, will make it easier for others to pay attention and train their eyes on you. It is all about how you can continue to bring your message across, by being conscious of how your body is moving.

How to Change Your Emotions at Any Time
The following process for changing mood and emotion should be done in a practice setting for a while so that you get the hgang of what to look for and hoe how to give your brain the cuese it needs to change. You need to comfortable in understanding what your exact cues are that your mind picks up on with any given emotional state.

• Straighten your back and eliminate any slouch in your stance, whether you are sitting or standing.

• Take deep and controlled breaths.

• Relax your facial muscles and put a smile on your face.

• Use a calm and upbeat tone when conversing with people.

Close your eyes and envision a calm and serene environment if possible. (This is not practical if you are driving, but you can always pull the car over and do this)

You will feel an immediate relief from depression, high anxiety or even anger. Your body is able to pick up on the cues you send it right away. When you practice, try placing yourself in a down emotion. All you have to do is use the normal physiology you would when feeling extremely tired or depressed. It works right away. Be sure and reintroduce a better and happier feeling before you move on with your day!

Brushing Away Negative Experiences
Imagine yourself sitting in the corner of a room. As you are reading this, imagine that you can feel the dampness of the cold cobblestone, and that feeling is so vivid you can even smell the pavement, as if it is covered in moss. In the distance you can hear tiny drops of water, trickling as if there is a leaking pipe somewhere in the dark. Suddenly, the light is switched off. You cannot see anything. But you can hear footsteps approaching. You know that a person is right in front of you. You feel that your hands are being tied by a rope, and you are being bound to your chair by that someone huge. And then, you feel that there is something crawling at on the back of your neck. It feels like a big spider.

How did that entire scenario makde you feel? It was rather uncomfortable, right? However, by now you know that you are back in your comfortable seat, reading this. You are safe from harm, but somehow, imagining that rather scary scenario happening to you gives you the creeps.

The same goes with your worst possible fear. At one point, you are certain that you have experienced the very reason why you would always dread being placed in a similar experience. Can you remember how you first encountered that fear?

Here is what you should keep in mind when it comes to control – mostly everything that is around you affects you to a certain degree, however, you can only manipulate how you react towards them. That means that you have total control over your thoughts and your emotions. That also means that the best way to make the best decisions in life is to always have reigns reigned over what you think and what you feel.

Things You Should Get Over With
When you want to make sure that you are getting what you want out of this life, there are two things that you should learn how to get rid of: harmful suggestion and fear. Why is that the case? Because the

negativity that you think exists is not real, but rather a manifestation of something that you can always get rid of.

You can think about the worst things that you have ever heard about you. Someone in the past might have called you ugly or fat, and he did it often enough that you never got his voice out of your head. One way or another, there is a memory that all want to simply erase. If they can't do that, they would want to make sure that it does not bother them anymore.

Dissociation

The bad idea that you have about your environment is part of the past, which is something that you are trying to avoid. You want to make sure that any bad incident would not happen again. However, by living with your fear and all the mean things that have been said to you before, you know that you are perpetuating something that you would very much like to avoid.

Don't get it wrong – there would be times when even your decision making is riddled with the worst bad thoughts or emotions, but you can still get to the conclusion that you want to arrive at. However, if you believe that a previous experience is a credible source of information for all the actions that you would be doing in the future, you might be wrong. While the experience can shape you, it would still depend on how you are going to interpret it.

Normally, this is what people do: they take their fears and negative experiences deeply in such a way that these become sensations that they associate with different objects and scenarios in their environment. They do it in such a way that they serve as a warning on how they would experience pain or defeat, and they do not want to touch or enter them. However, they are not even sure if these objects or scenarios would actually hurt them. They merely assume. Surely, you behave like these people at certain points.

However, the NLP technique called dissociation would help you cut away the emotions that you still experience by linking them with your previous unpleasant encounters. That means that whenever you feel angered or traumatized after you hear a particular word or see a particular object, you would be able to take control of those negative emotions.

Brushing Away Bad Thoughts

Why is it like that? It is because people can imagine the exact scenario where they have experienced fear or pain and try to imagine it as vividly as possible whenever they think that they are in a similar situation. They are watching the scene as if it is a life-size picture.

However, you can react differently. You can imagine that situation but this time, imagine it in a third person perspective, as if you are watching yourself via television. Now, remove the color from what you are watching. It feels like it is distant now. Then, make the television smaller, as if it is a size of a loaf of bread, but still, the scene does not have color. Afterwards, make it smaller and smaller, until it is the size of a breadcrumb. Since you can't see what's on the scene anymore, just brush it away.

How to Transform Bad Emotions into Good Ones

You know that you cannot get yourself to perform your best when you are in a foul mood, or when you are too distracted over the thought that you can possibly change. You sometimes feel that you would not be able to do anything that you wish you could, just because you feel anxiety over a situation. It is not because you have previously experienced failure in doing them. In fact, you might not have even tried it before. You just feel very anxious, to the point that you are reacting to the situation physically – your palms are sweating, and you feel that you are going to throw up.

Bad emotions most of the time stem from unpleasant situations that you have encountered before, which are so unpleasant that you are conditioned to always believe that the past is always bound to happen. You can sometimes imagine this: it is like being a kid again, trying to reason to your mother who would always tell you that you can't do anything right. She kept saying that over and over again for years that even now that you are living on your own, you can still feel that you are fighting for your right to do something you have always wanted. Well, you may think that your negative emotions are credible, but they are not – come to think of it, you are merely living with ghosts that you welcome inside your head.

Anchoring

When you feel that you are not ready to do anything you are supposed to do because of anxiety, anchoring can help you get over the negative sensations that you feel. Instead of fighting sensations that does not make sense, why not associate a different emotion, a positive one, to a situation that stresses you out?

Anchoring is all about associating a sensation with a particular stimulus, which would serve as the control inside your head. Your brain would think that the sensation and the stimulus work well together, and when the stimulus happens, the sensation will be felt. That way, you can always use the stimulus to feel something that can make you feel better.

For example, if you always feel anxious whenever you are required to speak to an audience, you think that the sensation that you MUST feel whenever you are with strangers is stress. However, what if you can replace the stress instead with excitement, which is something that you feel whenever you see your dog perfecting a trick? Here's how to do that:

1. Imagine seeing your dog in a movie screen, trying to do a trick, such as catch the ball. Beside you is a lever, which is connected to the screen.

2. Picture that the image you see on the screen is becoming more alive and in such great color that you think it is real. You begin to feel that you are getting excited, in such a way that you know that your dog would definitely be able to catch the ball and give it back to you the next time you throw it. To make yourself feel that sensation more, do the gesture – as if you are holding your dog's favorite chew ball.

3. Imagine that you are sliding up the lever, and that what it does is that it brings you closer to the screen, until you can almost feel that you are within the scene, but still, you are watching it. You can see every detail, and every color. You can almost hear your dog panting in anticipation of the ball you have in your hand. Hear a voice in your head, saying this: Let the fun begin.

4. Place the lever in its original position, after you have enjoyed the moment. You can feel that your body is beginning to associate the enjoyment with the task that you have to do. From now on, whenever you have to speak to a large group of people, you will feel the excitement that you felt during this exercise.

Here's another trick that you can do using NLP. You might be hearing yourself sometimes, saying that you cannot accomplish a task or that you must not try to join an activity because you do not have what it takes.

Imagine the voice that you hear inside your head. Is it the voice of someone you know? You probably would be hearing that bully who tormented you before, or that cynical teacher or boss who always doubted you. Now, transform that voice and turn it into a voice that you probably wouldn't hear firsthand in this lifetime, say Richard Nixon. You can also turn it into a voice that is so absurd that you wouldn't take anything that it is saying seriously, such as Donald Duck. Now, the hurtful things that you might find yourself saying that sometimes, you yourself saying against you would not matter, because you would hear them in the least believable way.

Amplify the Great Feeling
There are moments that you feel that you need to think happy

thoughts so that you can successfully achieve a goal. That can be your presentation that you are about to do in front of your big boss later, or that can be the marathon that you are about to run. What you think you should do is most likely the right thing – you know that whenever you are feeling great, you feel that you are unstoppable. Here's how you can grab on to the most positive feelings you can imagine.

1. Close your eyes. Think of the best experience that you have ever felt, that one that gave you the most impressive positive feeling you have ever had. Picture that experience and relive the sensations that you have felt. See what you have seen, and hear what you have heard.

2. As the great sensation flows into you, try to figure out where it starts. Is it coming from the top of your head or from your fingertips?

3. Cease thinking about that experience. Does the positive sensation immediately leave your body, or does it stay somewhere in your body?

4. Think about the positive experience again, and focus on the sensation it brings in. Just before the sensation leaves when your mind wanders to think of something else, e.g. your task at hand, pull the sensation back from that part of your body where you first experienced it. Keep doing that, until you feel that the sensation would keep looping all over your body, spinning faster and faster.

5. You would feel that the faster it spins and loops around your body, the stronger the positive sensation becomes. Now, you can enjoy the sensation while doing something else.

Now, you know that it is possible for you to control your emotions, and you realize that it is easy to get rid of the negative feelings that prevent you from looking at your environment the way it really is. You are also aware that it is possible for you to experience and emanate your positive emotions towards others. When you look at it, you can use that to your advantage to understand and influence others.

Chapter 9: Setting Goals for Ultimate Control

Neuro-Linguistic Programming is all about being able to set reasonable goals and reach them in a timeframe that you can handle. Since it only takes a few minutes a day there is no reason to not aim for progress every day. It can be done at home or at the office, so create a schedule that is easy for you to maintain.

If you notice very little change to begin with to revisit the list you created of by beliefs and see if any are emerging that you haven't addressed yet. It could be as simple as a limiting belief that you didn't catch the first time through. All you will have to do is follow the process to change it to a better and more beneficial belief.

A Still Mind Developed
The most important practice for the beginner, developing a still mind Here we will discuss the absolute most important practice for a beginner to learn how to affect their brains and their intimate experience of life.

The Breath
The most crucial aspect throughout our entire training is mastery of the breath. We must learn to keep our focus still on the breathing motion of the body. This is a fundamental skill of mind control discipline because we can utilize the breath to implant our thoughts with power. We must learn to still the mind and concentrate the breath to bring a clear point to our awareness from of where we may influence our self and our spirit.

Without the stillness realized through mastery of the breath discipline, in our efforts to influence ourselves, it would be as if we're attempting to place droplets of water into a raging river, the moment you release the droplet of water, it is gone, you will never ever see it again, it will be lost amidst the chaos and the effect that it could potentially have had on your life, mind and spirit will also be lost amidst the roaring torrent of a hundred thousand other thoughts.

To learn to watch the breath and utilize it for stilling and concentrating the spirit, is to learn to still the water and eventually it will be more like you are observing a still pond. Every one single drop of water that falls into that pond will create ripples and will in fact change the entire structure of the pond for a moment, the ripples spreading out across the entire surface in the form of beautiful symmetrical rings from its center.

To try to change your brain while your thoughts are a raging torrent is not difficult, it is rather impossible. It is the contents of the brain that are the focus for of most people's everyday life, they walk around thinking all day long about this or that, what is going to happen tomorrow, what happened yesterday, why he said that, why she did that, and it is that very process that develops certain patterns within its structure, resulting in what we call 'our-self' or 'our personality'.

It is that which we first must come to control and in fact, not really control, but let it die down, let it cease. We must learn to let go and find a place of stillness from which we can truly forge our lives with universal power, as opposed to the egoic intellect of the brain.

Step One – learn to watch the breath.
In your every waking moment you must learn to keep your attention on the breath and the body. This is meditation 101.
Learn to keep your attention moving around the breath and the body and you will see that the thoughts you previously paid so much attention to now no longer exist. They have never arisen due to the fact that your attention is now not focused in the brain, it is focused within your body and within your breath.

Here is the essential practice;
You can practice this exercise sitting, standing or laying down, walking, running, in fact in any place in any situation.

Technique 1- Learn to become a Watcher
• Hold your attention oin your breath

• Watch the in-breath and count to 3 for its duration

• Watch the out-breath and count to 3 for its duration

• Do this 10 times

• Technique 1.1 – Refine what it is that you are watching

• Hold your attention oin your breath

• Watch the in-breath and count to 3 for its duration

• Watch the moment between the in-breath and the out-breath, the pause at the top and count to 3 for its duration

• Watch the out-breath and count to 3 for its duration

• Watch the moment between the out-breath and the in-breath, the pause at the bottom and count to 3 for its duration

Both variations of this technique you must aim to practice for as long as possible. They will show you how, by changing what you are aware of, by taking your attention out of your brain and into your body, you will immediately find a release from the torrent of thoughts and you will begin to slow down, effectively changing your brainwaves.

Practice this during every waking hour if possible and learn how to become completely absorbed in the breath to the point where you feel full of air, like a large air balloon that is inflating and deflating with every breath.

You must learn to perform this practice completely and sincerely. You must master it. It is this essential practice that you will use to bring yourself back down to reality in later stages of practice. You are going to be learning some techniques that will have your brain spinning around like a hurricane, full of powerful and inspired thoughts, full of aims, goals, objectives and motivating emotions – believe me it will be a perfect storm, and you are going to need a way to bring that storm back down and return it to that of a still pond, from where it originated.

Technique 1.2 – Abdominal Breathing
In the same way that you are learning to keep out of the brain and stay focused within the body, now you must also break the habit of breathing from your lungs and learn to breathe from your abdomen.

Breathing from the abdomen has the effect of generating power, energy within the body, in the same way that spinning a gyroscope develops energy and that energy can, once built to a sufficient level, be attached to any and all other areas of our self- mastery discipline and will eventually turn our entire body into 'a manifestation machine' – quite literally this is the difference between using a single AA battery to light your torch and using 1 billion of them to light a lighthouse, one is going to illumine a much greater path than the other.

So you continue with the exact same practice as outlined above and now you are learning to keep your attention in your abdomen and breathe deeply and evenly from there the entire time.

Technique 1.3 – Stop Counting
Once you have genuinely practiced this technique to the point where you can literally focus for one hour without losing track and forgetting what you are doing, or without getting too lost in thought and giving up to go and do something else, you could be said to be proficient enough for the next step, which is quite simply to stop counting.

Now you can simply continue the exercise without counting to 3, but simply watching the in and out breath along with the space in between. You should still be forcing yourself to breathe deeply and by now you should be learning to breathe fully from your abdomen instead of your lungs.

Congratulations. At this point you have made great progress. Mastering this one technique will allow you to find a state of mind that is really very peaceful and unconcerned. After many years of intense practice in this specific technique you will come to know something about the nature of the breath that is really very profound and powerful. You must continue to practice this discipline for the rest of your life.

A Still Mind Maintained
The most important practice for an expert, maintaining a still mind
Now we will be considering walking through the world and maintaining your discipline. It is useless to develop such skill and mastery while sitting in your arm chair or lying down in your bed. You absolutely must forge your spirit and your mind in the fires of daily activity. You must learn to hold still as the eye of the hurricane so that when you are using your mind in the same manner that a master architect designs his labyrinths and palaces, so too you will be able to forge your entire existence without threat of distraction or destruction or infection (these three are one and the same).

These initial practices are the foundation for complete mastery of oneself. If they seem too simple to you, it is because you have not fully grasped the essence of what self-mastery is.

Self-mastery is very simply, complete control over your thoughts, behaviors and emotions to the point where absolutely every breath that you take is focused on some primary objective held still in mind.

That is it.
Anything else is watered down nonsense that people have used to hypnotize themselves into being able to change.

When you genuinely have the ability to hold your brain still and keep it focused on your objectives and keep it producing thoughts, behaviors and emotions that continuously push you in the right direction, to the exclusion of any negative thought, doubt, emotion or behavior, then the objective is complete and you have realized the initial phase of the training.

From there obviously you must live the rest of your life with such a mindset.

And that is where the real training will take place.

Technique 2 – Walking Through Stillness

While walking through the world you must be able to maintain a still mind. Your practice at this point in your training is to go about doing everything that you would normally do but while moving your attention throughout the following:

• Your breath

• Your physical body

• The things you can hear

• The things you can see

• The things you can smell

• The things you can feel

• The environment around you

Do not let your mind sit within the brain and allow thoughts to manifest. We are not yet at the point of consciously using thought as a tool for manifesting reality. We must first learn to hold to our state of stillness in any and all environments. This is done simply by being the master of what your attention is focused upon for the duration of every waking moment. If you find that you are still allowing your mind to stick to anything whatsoever, to the point where you fall back into the thought process, then there is more work to be done. You must be able to retire at the end of the day with the same still mind with which you awoke in the morning.

Do not rush this phase of the training. It is extremely important that you master this level of stillness. Without this, anything that you attempt to create later within your mind will be infected with the various slippages that will inevitably occur as the result of lack of mental discipline.

An example of this discipline may be as follows:

Pay attention to your breath.

After a brief moment move your attention to your feet.
After a brief moment move your attention to what you can hear.
After a brief moment move your attention to something that you can see.

After a brief moment move your attention back to the breath.
After a brief moment move your attention to the feeling of your scalp.
After a brief moment move your attention back to your right arm.
Etc, etc, etc

This practice will give you the ability to merge effectively with any situation you find yourself in, something that will be considered in
Once again, you must practice this discipline sincerely and completely otherwise true mastery will never be completely realized.

Forming the Self
The art of moving from stillness towards the forming of a self
From stillness, we may consider beginning to form within ourselves, a self. Once we have experienced a complete letting go of our old programming, due to consistent practice of the disciplines previously outlined, we may begin to forge within ourselves useful thought patterns and behaviors. To achieve this we can utilize a number of strategies.

1. Visualization

2. Pre-thinking

3. Internal Mental Barrier Construction

We will only discuss these three essential practices in this book. At this point in the training it is not necessary to outline the many variations of these three essential practices. We will simply introduce you to the concepts themselves and you can form any variations that you see fit to use.

Visualization
This skill is used to convince the brain that it is experiencing something that is not actually happening in the real world. To the brain, there is no real world, there is only information. Whatever information is passed along to the brain it uses to develop the body and personality associated with it.

Visualization should only ever be practiced in two specific modes;

• For a very brief instant as though dropping a stone into a still pond

• For an extended period of time, anywhere from 5 to 60 minutes

The essence of this practice is to use your imagination to experience the various scenarios and expectations that you wish to achieve or be a part of.

Use vivid colors to represent emotion and insert them into your mental images. Use sounds to enhance the experience and ensure that you cover all the sensory bases. Feel what it feels like inside your visualization and make it as vividly as you possibly can.

While practicing this technique for a very brief instant— You must develop the ability to contain a years' worthyears' worth of experience within a single thought. Imagine what it would feel like to have been living your ideal life, to have completely been the person you wish to be and to have achieved absolutely everything you want to achieve within a year from now, turn all of that information into a singularly condensed thought and feel it to be as powerful as it possibly can be while taking one full deep breath in and out, and then let it go and return to stillness to continue going about your daily activities.

Practicing this is like dropping a charged thought into the universal current of creation. It will sit and grow as a seed and eventually manifest within your thoughts and experience of life.

The essence of visualization has been presented to you here in this chapter. You must forge the ability to hold your minds steady on that which you visualize. No-one else in the world can do that for you.

Pre-thinking
The mind doesn't actually experience time. All that is known within the mind are the contents of the brain. Time is contained within those contents but the mind itself doesn't actually experience time, and so, whatever the contents of the brain are, the mind experiences now as now.

For example, to have a thought about the future, the mind sees this thought now. To have a thought about the past, the mind sees this now also. Becoming clearer?

Pre-thinking is the ability to place every encounter and every situation into the absolute best outcome you could possibly ever wish for, before allowing it to enter into your mind.

This is a difficult practice in some respects because it requires that you develop a very quick mental thinking faculty. You must be on top of your game, guarding your mind from any form of negative influence and ensuring that the entire contents of your mind are pointing towards, positivity, achievement, excellence, etc, things being exactly the way you want them to be in the future, but now.

It sounds a little complex but it isn't.
We are learning here that it is our thoughts that dictate anything and everything about our lives, so if we spare a single thought and allow our brains to begin focusing on any form of negativity whatsoever, for every second that we allow this to happen we are inspiring the growth of negativity and the ensuing misery within our minds. This simply will not do, in any circumstance, in any environment ever.

To master Prethinking is to be able to keep your brain focused at all times.

Internal Mental Barrier Construction
People use the expression, 'locked inside your mind', or 'mental barriers'. That is quite an interesting concept. Wouldn't you agree?

Imagine being caged within walls within your mind, so that every time you came to approach the barriers of your mind, certain behaviors would be triggered, certain thoughts or feelings would be set off and therefore keep you trapped within a certain outlook or belief system. Now that would be a very useful mental tool, don't you think?

To consciously develop mental barriers within our brains is a terribly stupid thing to do, unless we have the ability to break them apart as and when we choose.

This technique will develop an obsession within you. It will keep your mind constantly focused on whatever it is that are the main barriers you want to install.

For this technique you can attribute your mental barriers to a minimum of 1 concern and a maximum of 6 concerns.

I use the word 'concerns' here actively, because you are about to give yourself concerns, things that your mind is going to dwell upon and that will eventually cause you great strife, but is that not the function of mental barriers, to possess our thoughts and force us into certain behaviors and experiences? It's just that most people attribute mental barriers to negative things, here we will use them for inspiration, but believe me when I say, they are still concerns.

Once again, I reiterate that if you have not crystallized the ability to still your mind and remove any mental influences within your brain, you are going to send yourself psychotic if you practice this technique. You must know how to undo what you do, otherwise it will consume you. This I Promise.

Imagine yourself in a deep and dark abyss, with not a single point of light anywhere in your field of view. Now imagine your aim, as real as you possibly can, create it as vividly as you possibly can and immerse yourself in the experience – place everything in front of you and form it into a wall, a single wall.

This process should last at least 5 minutes.
Now repeat the process for every wall around you, even the floor and ceiling.

This should take at least a further 30 minutes

If you are doing this for only one objective, then reiterate it in every direction one wall at a time. If you are doing this for multiple objectives, then divide the walls up evenly or place your main priority within a larger number of walls.

Now you have created a hell for yourself. But as the story goes, the devil can have whatever he wants.

Your thoughts will stay confined within these mental barriers in your brain and you will have forced yourself to stay focused upon whatever objectives you have instilled within those walls.

But be warned.
If you allow your mind to slip even for an instant while performing the visualizations or if it slips after you have completed them, cracks will form in those walls and who knows what terrors may crawl inside from the eternal abyss, lying just inches on the other side.

If you rush past the initial stages of this training and attempt to practice these techniques without the proper level of stillness, you are inviting your subconscious mind to manifest all sorts of wonders and terrors that are quite simply, beyond your control.
As a master of true NLP, nothing should be beyond your control.

Don't rush!

Empty Face
The final aim of true Self Mastery – to crystalize the Heart of Mastery and realize the ultimate Empty Face Discipline.

To comprehend fully, the nature of Empty Face Discipline is to comprehend the ultimate mystery in all corners of the Cosmos. It is to comprehend the subtle reality of the breath and its essence. It is to realize complete, independent liberation and true self-mastery. This state has never been attained by anyone alive. It is impossible to describe the method of realizing Empty Face Discipline because there is in fact no technique. There is nothing you can do to attain it. It is the ultimate letting go of all impulse, all forms of mind, all forms of cognition and all form of thought. Empty Face Discipline is the home of the Supreme Self Mastered Spirit. It is the seat of the One who knows completely and utterly where his Heart is at, at all times and where his Mind is kept, at all times. There is no greater objective in all forms of NLP, Hynpnosis & Mind Control training. This is as far as it goes.

Black Mind

A wise man once wrote a book called Thick Black Theory. It was originally banned when it was published in 1911 and came to light only recently. This chapter will be an explanation and the evolution of that Grand-Master Strategy of NLP.

This is a difficult state of mind to master. It requires years of focused study and effort.

The original title outlined in the introduction to this chapter, Thick Black Theory is a book about Grand-Master Strategy in Mind Control.
 To understand the fundamentals of that book is to comprehend the essence of true mind control.

I will explain it in greater detail here.

In the same way that a Black Hole lets out no light, a Black Mind lets in no information.

A Black-Hole works in the way that it sucks everything in and lets out a constant stream of emptiness, pure space without form.
Black Mind works in complete balance to a Black Hole. Not one single thread of information will take root in your Mind. The only thing that you will express and you will express it constantly, is the contents of your own programming, that which you are working on developing and maintaining in your own life, your own way.

You will ignore peoples' statements about anything that is not relevant to your objectives. You will crush any information or doubt that people present to you. Absolutely nothing gets in.

This is a very difficult mindset to master and requires years and years of intense discipline in the first outlined techniques to fully assimilate.

This kind of mindset is something that will eventually overcome everything you have previously ever thought about NLP or influence. It will become something that you express constantly and will set you well on your way to realizing Empty Mind Discipline.

Heavy Heart
To crystalize the Heart of Mastery takes at least 10 years of practice. This chapter will discuss the process of crystalizing NLP within the heart and the strategies that are most effective for that.

Heavy Heart strategy is terrible. It really is. You will take the entire force of the universe and you will contain it in your Heart. You will walk everywhere throughout the world and you will hold this power within yourself. This is the space where you finally come to know the essence of the training. The whole point here is to realize such a level of discipline that you know nothing other than Self Mastery in your every waking moment.

At all times in the day you are to keep your attention focused oin the Heart. No matter what you encounter and what situation arises, you always keep your attention concentrated in the Heart.

This is the way of crystalizing mastery over the Mind via the essence of the Heart.

Once a Heavy Heart is realized, there is no more space for fear, no more space for doubt and there is no more space for confusion in the mind. Anything and everything that you encounter becomes a solid and a real part of yourself. You are able to firmly bring any project at all within your grasp and you can apply yourself to it completely and utterly without delay while knowing instantly and immediately what is the correct course of action to take to realize complete success.

The Heavy Heart is a technique of Empty Face Discipline. It is one of the most powerful techniques, yet it cannot be called a technique. It is a realization that occurs within the Spirit and it brings the practitioner bordering on the realms of real intimate knowledge of the fundamental workings of the universe.

Create a List for an Expected Outcome
In order to give your path real direction you need to sit down and write out a list of goals. The ultimate goal with NLP is called outcome. What are the behaviors you want to change or the emotional controls that you want to put in place. How do you envision your life being different or improved? It will save you from taking a lot of unnecessary steps. It will help you focus your energies to on what really matters.

If you are trying to change negative behaviors, then you spend a good amount of time exploring what the emotions are behind the behavior. Many people that smoke are not just fighting a physical addiction. Cigarettes are often used as a way to combat stress and anxiety. This means that the desired outcome would be to quit smoking, but it will entail first getting a grip on high levels of stress and anxiety.

How do your beliefs match up with your desired outcome? You need to have absolutely no doubts about your abilities to reach your end goal. If you see any stumbling blocks take care of them as soon as possible. If you are battling depression, it may take seeking assistance with medications and therapy. If you are trying to combat an addiction it may take a short in-patient treatment to start. You always need to make sure that you are doing things safely and using common sense. Give yourself every chance to succeed.

An easy way to ensure that you have everything you need on the list is to use the power of visualization. Here, you begin by picturing the end result of what you want to achieve, and the joy that you will experience once it is achieved. The next thing you need to do is to think of all the steps that you need to take in order to get to that end result. It is from evaluating these steps that you will be able to create a list of tasks that need to be completed.

Determine What the Path to Change Requires
If you struggle with anger management then it only makes sense that certain situations will predispose you to losing your temper. Some people refer to these as "pet peeves." Learning to avoid them when possible, or at least limiting the importance they hold to creating your emotional state is needed. If you can recognize that you tend to like controlling every type of situation you are that much farther ahead. You cannot possibly always have control and you have to practice letting that go.

If you need to get control over depression you need to see where your mind tends to wander during periods of rest. Many people suffering from depression are very caught up worrying about things that cannot be controlled. Feeling as if you have no power in a given situation can lead to serious bouts of depression.

Concentrate on things about a situation that you CAN control. If you have a troubled marriage spend time doing things during the day that you enjoy. Every bit of momentary happiness you can bring into your life will make the rest seem a bit more bearable.

If you are dealing with anxiety start a worry journal. It needs to be a notebook that you set aside to put all of your worries into. It will allow your mind to stay less absorbed with troubles that bring about high stress and feelings of anxiety. Let your mind know that you will simply look it over and worry about things later. It will bring about a state of relaxation and help you get control of unexpected and harsh bouts of anxiety.

It may take seeking the help of a professional to get down to what emotions are driving you to do unwanted behaviors. Once you know the cause, you can work on the cure. When it comes to emotional control, you will see improvement in a matter of weeks by being consistent.

If for any reason you are unable to see a professional, you can still find ways to address and deal with these types of emotions. You should start by taking time to understand really what path you are currently on, and why there seems to be a problem If all goes well, people are normally not interested in correcting a plan, but if just one thing goes wrong, there can be serious panic.

The most important thing about using NLP to deal with this situation is to be honest with yourself and look objectively at your path. This will make it easier for you to recognize and initiate any changes that are necessary.

Create Your Personal Milestones
If you took a road trip across the United States starting in New York and ending up in California, the trip would be more pleasant if you took breaks occasionally. Going from point "A" to point "B" can be a stressful journey if the end point is a long distance. It is no different if you are aiming for a very high goal. You will find success easier to reach if you break things up into mini-goals or milestones.

Milestones also include criteria that can be set out at the beginning of the journey, to provide a plan of action in regards to the goal to be met. They can also act as stops along the way where you can reward yourself, especially if most of the work that one dies in mental rather than physical.

Changing behaviors or emotional controls can seem overwhelming initially. Change is not always an easy thing to do. Breaking it all down into pre-planned bite size portions can help. It allows you to implement ultimate focus on each leg of the journey. If you are trying to quit a bad habit and over-reach it can cause complete failure. Once again, we will point towards cessation of smoking as an example. The quitting cold turkey method works for a few, but very few. Why is that? It is a drastic all or nothing approach. Allow your body time to reduce in nicotine levels so that you can better deal with the psychological addiction that smoking holds.

This is another reason why NLP is so successful. The ability to personalize every step on your path allows you to design a way to initiate change that makes it hard to fail. You can speed up the process, slow down or go back to square one, and you will never lose any of the positive benefits you have already received.

Establishing a Better Future

Can you think of the biggest problem that you have right now? If yes, how much time do you spend trying to imagine how your life can be worse if you do not solve that problem? You are probably spending several hours worrying about that.

When you think about it, there are a lot of hours in a day that you spend on useless things – you crave for food that is bad for you, you have your vices, and then you spend more time wondering what is going to happen with your life now that your liver and heart feels that they are going to fail in two years. Somehow you know that there is a simple solution to that problem. However, you spend more hours whining how hard it is to accept that that is the only logical answer to your woes.

So what are you doing, essentially? You are prolonging your agony, and then you imagine yourself resigning to the idea that you are bound to fail. Or, you would pray that you will get over all those difficulties, but you cannot think of any alternative solution that you would probably like better.

Do Not Worry

What do you get when you worry? You feel that you are way worse than how you really are, and when you start getting to the worst part of your imagination, you will soon feel that the world is ending. In reality, that is not the case. In reality, all your problems have really simple solutions.

If you think that you are stuck with a problem, stop whatever you are doing, look at the situation from another perspective, and then think of another way to solve it. If you keep on carrying out the solution that you think would work, you would not be able to arrive at the conclusion you are aiming at. Worrying that you would never be able to finish your task will never be useful as well. All you need is to do something else that you are certain would work.

If you are certain that what you are doing is not working, think that there is always an easier way. First, change your internal state. Relax and stop that voice inside your head that tells you that you only know one way of doing things, and it is not working. When you are able to do that, you will be able to look at yourself and your task from another perspective.

Change Your Belief

All the things that you know now are products of a lengthy process of continuous learning. The things that you know how to do are learned, and so are your beliefs. They are all products of your engagement with your environment. Now, when your environment changes and the knowledge that you have about the world seems to be lacking, you have to adapt.

Beliefs become knowledge and there's a logical explanation for the world around you because you can provide justifications. You cannot believe that Pluto is a planet when there is evidence that that is a false claim. If you cannot think how a belief system would possibly help you in a situation, it is alright for you to change it and conform to a new one. As long as the world changes, it is only logical for you to keep switching beliefs.

Your thoughts would be actions, and then they become habits. The moment that you are capable of changing how you think, you can stop having those bad habits that you have. What you think becomes who you are. Remember that if smokers forget what a cigarette is, they will forget the entire habit of smoking. So if you stop telling yourself that you are incapable or unworthy, you would have a different belief system about yourself.

You are Not a Product of Your Past

You may believe that your future is a product of your past – that is not necessarily true. In order for you to have total control of your actions and be convinced that you can always change for the better, remember that your future is not dictated. You may have been catering to beliefs because of previous experiences, but recognize that you can choose how the past can affect you. You are not supposed to only rely on what you already know. You have to rely on the current things available for you now, because they are quite different from the resources that you have had before.

Being able to recognize that opportunities and life in general change constantly allows you to be aware that you do have mental faculties that allow you to replace the bad characteristics that you have and replace them with the right behavior that will actually help you. They allow you to recognize which goals are still relevant, and they remind you that you are capable of progressing from one ideal to another. They allow you to be the person that you want to be, despite the ideal personality that society thinks is the right fit for you. Knowing that you are not only made of the merits you already have allows you to be in control and to grow.

Understand the Relationship bBetween Your Mind and Body

Do you notice that your body also responds to your mindset? When you are feeling under the weather, your posture stoops and you feel that your face sags. The opposite happens when you are experiencing pleasant emotions. However, the reverse also works – when you are uncertain of how you can change your internal state, work it out using your body. If you are feeling down or anxious, fix your posture and assume a confident stance. You will be surprised how you would feel better afterwards!

Chapter 10: Recognizing Success

How will you know when NLP has worked? The visible signs of a change in behaviors and feeling more in control of your emotions are well and good, but there are other ways that you can feel successful along the way. The one thing that will immediately and forever improve is your self-awareness of both mood, emotional control and how it impacts any behaviors you exhibit.

A first method you can use to check the success of your NLP is to observe the way other people are reacting to you. Has it improved communication? Are they looking up to your more? Have you heard a comment that something about you is "different"? If people are reflecting back positivity to you whenever you have an interaction with them, it is quite likely to evidence you need in order to believe that NLP is working.

Being able to master your emotions at any given time is a way of controlling situations that you may have never enjoyed before. You will fully realize the truth of the saying "you cannot control others, but you can control how you react to things." It is empowering.

There is very little that will bother you once you learn the process of taking care of your own emotional health.
In fact, numerous researchers and educators have spoken about controlling emotions in order to move ahead in life. There will always be a critic or a judge, but practicing NLP will give someone more confidence in themselves and what they can achieve. It teaches a sense of responsibility and avoids the impact of laying blame on other parties.

Once you have changed the beliefs in your subconscious mind, you will not take unexpected trips backward in progress. Your subconscious mind will put every effort into pushing the conscious mind to meet your goals. As easy as it used to be to ride on an emotional roller coaster you will feel the ability to take control and get into calmer and peaceful states allowing them to take over. The real success lies in taking the necessary time to find the bad beliefs and change them.

The 4 Principles of Success
NLP has various techniques that can create behavioral changes and improvements, all geared towards the achievement of success. However, these techniques are guided by the four operational principles of NLP. These are:

• **Knowing the outcome you want to achieve**

• Having sufficient sensory acuity

• Having sufficient flexibility of behavior

• Taking action now

Knowing the outcome you want to achieve
NLP gives great emphasis on the importance of outcomes. This is because outcomes serve as the objective and overall mission of every NLP technique. No NLP intervention can move forward without a proper outcome. Some people are either unaware of their desired outcomes or afraid to formulate them at all. Some people are more focused on the avoidance of things they do not want. Most people on the other hand have outcomes they have identified but are poorly stated. This results to in an outcome that loses its intended purpose of motivation and most importantly, a capacity to focus.

Having no outcomes in life is dangerous because you will go about your life without any purpose or passion. Having an outcome that is more concerned on the avoidance rather than achievement creates a bleak and miserable life. Having an outcome that is poorly formulated can derail you from tapping your potential.
NLP recommends certain conditions that will allow you to create the most appropriate outcomes in your life. There are variations on how to formulate a correct outcome; some make use of the 5 well-formed conditions while others use the SMART method.

The 5 conditions are: positivity, testable by the senses, sensory specific, initiated and sustained by the person, contextualized and ecologically sound. Positivity means that your outcome must be stated in terms that are reflective of an achievement, not avoidance or doing something instead of not doing something. For example, a negative outcome is, "Not eating too much junk food." A positive outcome is, "Eating healthy foods."

Testable by the senses means you can measure your progress and achievement and use the measurement as proof of attaining the outcome, "Eating healthy foods that are within the daily nutritional requirement of 1000 calories per day."

Sensory specific means that you can verify the success of the achievement of the outcome using your senses, "Eating healthy foods that are within daily nutritional requirement of 1000 calories per day and resulting to an ideal body weight of 60 kilos."

Initiated and sustained by the person means that you have to personalize and take responsibility of the outcome rather than depending on others to achieve it for you, "I will be eating healthy foods that are within my daily nutritional requirement of 1000 calories per day and resulting to an ideal body weight of 60 kilos."

Contextualized means that the outcome must be able to exist in the person's own environment and time frame, "For 6 months, I will be eating healthy foods that are within my daily nutritional requirement of 1000 calories per day and resulting to an ideal body weight of 60 kilos."

Finally, ecologically sound means that you have to take into consideration how your outcome, not only affects yourself but also other people in your environment, "For 6 months, I will be eating healthy foods that are within my daily nutritional requirement of 1000 calories per day. I will do this until I achieve my ideal body weight of 60 kilos. When I am successful in this outcome, this will create healthy relationships, both for myself and provide security and confidence to those around me."

Notice the difference with the first poorly constructed outcome of "Not eating too much junk food" and the more appropriate statement of the outcome of "For 6 months, I will be eating healthy foods that are within my daily nutritional requirement of 1000 calories per day. I will do this until I achieve my ideal body weight of 60 kilos. When I am successful in this outcome, this will creates healthy relationships both for myself and provide security and confidence to those around me."

Another alternative is the 5 SMART methods. It is an acronym that stands for specific, measurable, achievable, realistic and timed. Some NLP trainers make use of the SMART method because it is easier to remember and apply. However, the end result of using this method is still very similar to the first 5 conditions. The important thing in knowing your outcome is not which conditions or methods that you will use but the outcome must have characteristics that are positive, motivating, purposeful and most importantly focused.

Having Sensory Acuity

Sensory acuity refers to the principle that gives importance to your ability to observe another person. Particularly, you are interested in discerning his communication, both verbal and non-verbal, as clues to his thought processes. NLP believes that even a person's innermost thoughts that may be consciously or unconsciously repressed are revealed by a person's behavior.

In NLP, the spoken word only accounts for 7% of the total message. The tone of the voice with its quality, speed, pitch and volume accounts for another 38% of the communication. This why much can be hidden from another person because most people rely on hearing the words only instead of using the full senses to understand what the other person is trying to communicate or trying to hide.

The bulk of true communication lies ion the physiology of the communicator, it accounts for 55% of the entire message. This is where the concepts of body language are valuable. NLP teaches practitioners the way to consolidate both verbal cues, provided by the spoken word and the tone of the voice and the non-verbal cues, evidenced by posture, facial expression, blinking, gestures and breathing.

This principle provides a wealth of insights for NLP practitioners, particularly in relating with other people. First, this provides them with the ability to determine consistency between what they hear versus what they see in a person. For example, your client is telling you that business deal will push through as planned. However, you hear in his voice a lowered volume as he speaks and you see a barely noticeable restlessness that betrays his unease on your conversation. Instead of accepting his statement, you are prompted to make further inquiries or probe him on the veracity of his claim.

Secondly, sensory acuity allows you to increase your sensitivity towards people around you. Remember, your behaviors are part of a sub-system or a greater ecology. This means that with or without knowing it, you are affecting the people around you. You can gauge your effect by analyzing and interpreting their communication using your full range of senses. For example, you are at a gathering with your family and distant relatives. You notice a subtle change in their behavior as you move from one table to another. This gives you a clue that you are creating an unintended effect and must prompt you to review your behavior.

Finally, this principle teaches you the success of your attempts to influence the behavior of another person. If you are actively trying to persuade a person to do something, then you must be able to verify his change with his behavior. For example, you are trying to sell a product to a customer. The customer tells you that he will make a purchase but you notice that he constantly averts his eye from meeting yours. He folds his arms around his chest and clenches his fist underneath. These gestures indicate a discrepancy between his words and his true message, which is indicative of your lack of rapport. This is the feedback that you did not reach your desired outcome.

Having Sufficient Flexibility of Behavior
This principle is closely related to the Law of Requisite Variety. This states that in the every changing world that constantly incorporates changes to restore balance; you must have a wide range of

behaviors to still remain successful. You need to be open to new options, strategies and concepts to address changes in your life as they occur. You cannot be stuck with an all-in-one solution or method to achieve success. If in case the feedback you receive does not allow you to attain success, you must be ready with another method. You need to vary your behavior until you attain the outcome you desire.

For example, you are trying to change the behavior of your partner from being too suspicious of your private affairs, to become more trustful, and have more faith in you. You behave by calling her from time to time to let her know where you are but still she is suspicious. You bring her with you whenever possible, which she appreciates but with sensory acuity, you know that her perception remains unchanged.

You initiate a new behavior, this time you explore into her verbal and non-verbal messages and find out that she had a colored past with another person which resulted to her persistent suspicion. You tell her that you are not that person and commit to never becoming that person; you become successful in changing her behavior.

On a deeper application of this principle, NLP recommends that if one NLP technique does not provide the outcome you desire, then it may mean that the technique is inappropriate for the problem. Choose another technique until you achieve the outcome.

Chapter 11: Taking Action Now

This is the final principle of NLP and its simplicity must not be thought of holding less importance. This principle, equally important as with the first three, simply means that NLP practitioners believe that success can truly be achieved not only by knowledge but also by the **manifest application of knowledge through action.** NLP gives no place for complacency and procrastination. In fact, it is all about active participation, taking control and becoming assertive. It is not only about introspecting on your thoughts and the words you use, but also taking concrete actions towards the achievement of your outcome.

This final principle is the inspiration for the succeeding chapter in this book. Each NLP technique discussed will be a combination of information (knowledge) and instructions for application of the knowledge (action). Take note that NLP techniques are constantly being added or improved in respect to the Law of Requisite Variety.

Remember the presupposition that **there is no failure, only feedback.** There is no failed technique, there is only a mismatch. Use the presuppositions and the principles to motivate you towards applying these techniques, barring away failure and achieving the success you truly deserve.

Chapter 12: Practical Application of Neuro Linguistic Programming

"Questions are also interventions. A good question can take a person's mind in a completely new direction and change his life. For example, ask yourself frequently, 'What is the most useful question to ask now?"

John Seymour

Emotions in Relationships

When you learn to use Neuro Linguistic Programming techniques, you can take a difficult situation and look at it from all kinds of perspectives, helping you to make decisions that affect your life. For example, you are in a marriage and are unhappy with the way that the marriage is going. You have choices left open to you. You can continue to be sad within that marriage, you can find out what it is that makes the marriage unhappy or you can look beyond the marriage to see whether divorce or separation is a potential answer to your problems. Of course, people make decisions like this every day, though Neuro Linguistic Programming helps you to see situations more objectively.

In the above case scenario, there are the feelings of others to consider. The picture is bigger than how the subject in the scenario feels. Any decision will have an impact on everyone. It's like a row of dominoes where one is tipped and all the others follow in turn. Using Neuro Linguistic Programming methods, you can anticipate the fall of the dominoes and are able to make your decisions based on a wider perspective.

Every event in life can be seen from different perspectives. If you are told that your house is going to be repossessed, the automatic response to that would be negative. You may think things such as:

I am going to lose my home

I will have nowhere to live

I have nowhere to put my belongings

These are all negative thoughts, which won't help the situation. The fact is that you are going to lose your home, and will have to look beyond that to find something new so that you do have a roof over your head. The Neuro-Linguistic approach means that instead of looking at the situation as being totally negative, you take the positive route and that this helps you to be more open to positive suggestion and positive results.

The house was falling down anyway

This will put an end to my debt

This gives me a chance for a new start

All of these are positive reactions and give you the potential of finding solutions that you won't find if you let negative thoughts take over. Although this case scenario may be a little drastic, the day to day events that you face in life can similarly be faced in a way that gives you more choices, rather than less. The more choices you allow yourself through your practice of Neuro Linguistic Programming, the more likely you are to leave yourself open to opportunity.

It is impossible to have a book about emotion and transforming behavior without touching on the most important emotion of them all, and that is love. NLP techniques can bring about highly successful relationships, as each person is the relationship can work on their self-esteem and perfect some excellent communication skills.

NLB also helps with acceptance of a relationship and in helping the parties widen their perspectives when dealing with each other.
To make NLP work in your relationships, you can try the following steps: -

• **Know what you believe**
You need to develop more than just a positive though, you need a positive belief. This means that you believe in the possibility of having a brilliant relationship and that you will find the right person for you. Positive thinking can only have one output, and that is a positive result. With this belief will come the motivation to go out and look for the relationship that you want (that is if you are single). If you are in a relationship, you should be encouraged to make improvements to your relationship.

• **Make a non – negotiable list**
There are qualities that you will be looking for in a partner, and criteria for what is important to you. These are called your non-negotiables, meaning that if they are missing, you would seriously consider the viability of the union.

Using NLP, you will be able to discern which of these criteria is are most important to you. When speaking to the person you desire, you can mentally check whether they meet your pre-determined criteria.

While doing so, you should also attempt to see them from their own perspective. You may even find yourself amending your life as you go along.

• Actively Communicate

One of the maxims of NLP is that you cannot not communicate. Therefore, be proactive and communicate with the one who is the center of your attention. Whether you choose to communicate through the phone, email or even text messages, take time to find out more about the other person. This should help to increase your motivation.

• Avoid Arguments

Arguments and misunderstanding can be the downfall of any relationship, no matter how healthy it appears to be. With NLP techniques in mind, it becomes much easier to avoid arguments when dealing with your partner.

The best technique to use is pacing and leading. This directly relates to how one listens to their partner and then how they choose to react when dealing with a conflict. The listening should allow for adequate time to process what is being said, and leading should steer the conversation towards a solution for the problem.

• Set SMART goals

NLP is all about setting goals, and visualizing where you would like to be in the future. The same principles can apply to relationships, so that it becomes easier for you to assess whether the relationship is working. That is why it is imperative to set SMART goals.

• See the world through the eyes of others

People like to be right about a whole range of things, but most particularly, this can become evident when dealing with their point of view. The great thing about NLP is that it makes one aware of all the filters that make it difficult to see a clear line. These filters may carry the values and expectations that have been accumulated over the years.

By understanding these filters, it becomes much easier to deal with people's behavior. There is also an incredible amount of patience, as a person without NLP will find that they may not be able to communicate with everyone due to quirks in the personality.

These maps in the mind form an understanding of how the world will be used and seen. A good communicator would be someone that is able to mentally move from their own map to match their partners map, making it easier for to better understand each other.

• It's not just the message, it's the response.

If you have heard the term lost in translation, then you know that a message can lose all its meaning, all because it has been misunderstood. The normal result would be to blame the people around for this bad result.

NLP gets rid of the blame game completely. The person relaying the message is responsible for how it is understood. Therefore, if the message is not clear the one who is listening takes no blame, while the person passing forward the message would need to repeat or improve upon what they communicate.

NLP makes it possible to "speak the other person's language" when communicating. This means that there is enough flexibility, which can allow for improved communication.

• Do your best with what you have
The atmosphere around relationships is charged with expectations. There are expectations on both sides, mixed with emotions.

It is important to use NLP to understand the reason that people will behave in the way that they do, looking at their behavior and concluding that there is always a positive intention. It is all about patiently changing perspective, and appreciating that your partner is doing the best that they can with the resource that are available in at that moment.

Other NLP skills in Relationships
A practical application of NLP in a relationship is to use your auditory skills. This involves being able to truly listen to your partner. When you choose to actively listen, you can learn inspiring and amazing things about your partner. It also makes it easier for you to establish a rapport with them.
Creating a powerful visual image of your partner can do wonders for your love life. This involves visualizing them as you would like to see them, smiling, laughing, flirting and being happy.

To enhance your love, you can try this exercise.

• This exercise is meant to diffuse an argument. To start, you need to picture a time when you and your partner had a lovely day together. Focus on the rapport you built, and the intensity of your feelings.

• Remember the sounds you heard, the sights you see, tastes and smells you experienced and the touch you shared.

• Once you are fully in the moment, anchor it to any part of your body.

• Next, recall a time you had an argument. Think of about your tone of voice, the surrounding area, and picture it as a still black and white picture.

Anchor this and fire it, letting it go.

Chapter 13: Transformation in Business

Companies around the globe have started to adopt NLP practices because they have incredible benefits that can propel the company to the next level. At the most basic, using NLP techniques will almost guarantee an increase in sales. In addition, communication between colleagues can improve vastly. All round, NLP is just what a business needs.

Neuro Linguistic Programming has a range of dimensions which are applicable in business. These include handling motivation patterns, behavioral change technology, conflict resolution, training, and coaching, influencing and learning and teaching. All these dimensions deal with emotions at some level, and once managed, these emotions are of great benefit.
The following section is intendeds to address how NLP can build a business by optimizing its total performance.

Understanding What You Want
One of the biggest challenges that you will face in any career that you choose is finding out if what you choose to offer to the public is something that you yourself would want. Is the product or service that you are trying to profit from going to make you feel fulfilled? Do you think that you can operate this business for a long time?

Being able to know what you want would require you to tap on your values. As a rule, people would always want to set high standards for themselves, because they would not want to be stuck in a rut and then feel that life is stagnant. They would always want to find healthy challenges, but they do not want to feel that they are going against their values. For this reason, people would always find that something is worth doing if it goes well with their core beliefs. They feel that what they are aiming to do provides them purpose, and at the same time, possible success.

When you want to influence people to adhere to your policies or believe in the products you offer, it is very important that you actually believe that they are actually beneficial – it has to show that you are using it, or at least think that that product can make the world better. The reason for that is that it would be hard to lie when you are not convinced that what you are offering is something important. When you are convinced that what you offer is something that would just generate money, but definitely of no importance at all, your body language will begin to give clues that you do not believe in the importance of what you are offering. Your shoulder stoops, your voice shakes a bit, your eyes feel blank or look like they are trying to avoid the other person's gaze. Here's the thing – the way you behave would matter more than what you say, and more often than not, that is the key to a sale.

Of course, there are people who are perfectly great at selling something that they do not even use. You might believe that being able to memorize spiels or being able to write a great copy about your products and services would let you get away with it. You may become successful at controlling your body language, but would you wouldn't want to be always conscious about how you act. At the same time, you would also want to grow a business or be in an industry that you would not want to quit after some time. You would want to be passionate about your career.

Making Yourself Fit for Business

What is the best way to guarantee success after you have determined what you want to get out of your endeavors? You need to ensure that you are equipped to move towards achieving your goals. However, having the confidence to believe in ones' self is something that not everybody is trained for. There are people who think that they have experienced something in the past that makes them fail every time they move towards their goal. Some blame it to their upbringing, their educational background, or the lack of enthusiasm from people around them. In essence, there are a lot of people who think that they need the proper support system in order for them to reach their goals.

However, there are people who only count on themselves in order for them to achieve success. More often than not, these people are able to make their first million sooner than they think. They believe that they need others to persevere, but they take on the leadership role. They simply believe that they have to make the proper steps in order to convince people to support them. They put ion the extra hours in order for them to prove to others that they are worth their time. They did not need to lean too much on what they have learned from school or what they have inherited from their parents. They think that they are capable of changing in order for them to receive the rewards they work hard for.

In a sales environment

If a salesman telephones a potential lead and gets a negative response, it's usually because the approach is incorrect. The salesman has givengave the impression he has something for sale that a client, for his own reasons, does not want to buy. If you take this as fact, then you actually limit the potential of selling. Neuro Linguistic Programming tools would have stopped you from making that unsuccessful call in the first place. You would have had more insight into what your potential customers want, you would also know what the competition has to offer and would be able to offer potential clients something they can't get anywhere else. Thus, this system is taught to businesses worldwide, to help them gain success.

Optimizing Organizational Performance
NLP can make an impressive difference when the people in any business apply its techniques. This is because, with an active practice of NLP, it is possible to change behavior in such a way that everyone ius working towards achieving success.

Optimizing One's Self
Neuro linguistic programming is technically geared to boost one's emotional intelligence, simply because people do not function their best when they feel down. Without the necessary emotional capacity to work, people are bound to half-heartedly go to their jobs, and their performance shows it. It is a basic necessity for any person to feel that his work is rewarding, and that he can get fulfillment out of his career experience so that he would look forward to doing the same thing the next day. For that reason, bosses give incentives. The same logic is followed in sales – a seller needs to make the buyer think that buying a product today will bring him numerous rewards, or at the very least, it would make him happier.

At this point, you should ask yourself this: do you feel that the things that you do every day is bringing you satisfaction? If you know that the end result of the career that you are in would be something that you truly desire, then you should not have any problem with waking up early mornings, driving your car to work, and presenting to clients. You should think that while you may lack some life experiences when it comes to selling or managing a firm, you are optimistic that you would have the opportunity to get them, as long as you keep doing what you do. At the same time, you would also feel confident that you could keep on learning and changing in order for you to get the results that you want.

There is a reason why people have the capacity to be more influential than others – they believe that they have the power to do so. There are people that can survive any situation they are in as long as they are in the company of others. They manage to convince others that they can do anything together, and that they can profit from it. Some have the ability to make others see that a partnership with them can provide them leverage. With such a simple belief in the self, these people make good managers or company owners. If they are working for others, they would make good marketers or they will be great in a sales team. With their ability to sell themselves more than they can sell the products that they offer, they can be placed in any job possible. That is because they have the ability to make others listen and believe in them.

To start off, there are four principles that can guide any business interested in achieving success. The four principles are:

a) Work to Achieve Outcomes

Active use of NLP requires a person to begin to set goals, and work towards attaining those goals. This is particularly applicable in a business setting. Once you have an idea of what your outcome should be, your mind is better able to process the steps that should be taken so that you can meet that outcome. The key, and this is where NLP becomes effective, is to be conscious of your actions.

Being conscious can help your business stand out from a range of other businesses out there. Rather than working towards what they want, businesses not familiar with NLP might be working to avoid what they do not want. The problem with working with a negative outlook is that you will always attract a negative outlook. NLP places great emphasis on being outcome-oriented and focused. It also preaches positivity and suggests that even negative actions could have positive intentions.

In order to achieve these outcomes, it is important they are stated in positive terms. This means that they should always be skewed towards the 'bright side', instead of things that cannot get done.

To ensure that your projected outcomes are viable, they must be testable and measurable in a sensory specific way. This means that there should be some evidence to prove the outcome has been met. Being sensory specific means that you should be able to express yourself with words and feelings should you achieve the outcome.

When working towards achieving an outcome, it must be initiated and maintained by one person. This person needs to be in control of the outcome from beginning to end so that the behavior can be monitored, and changes made if necessary. The idea here is that through NLP, an individual within the business can initiate a wave of positive change through their own behavior. It also makes it easier for them to be held accountable for their actions ...... or to get a bonus.

Every action has an equal or positive reaction. By practicing NLP, you become aware of your actions and their possible consequences to ensure that no harm comes to you or other people. You are also better able to project positive actions, so that if people are mirroring back what they see in you, you will only have positive responses to content with.

b) Understand and Be Aware of your Senses

When you have mastered the ability to use NLP, you will be able to read other people easily. This refers to all the non-verbal cues they use consciously or unconsciously when communicating with you. Your senses should be heightened because you are more aware of them.

You should be able to notice changes in skin color (blushing or going pale), higher or lower breathing rates, and even any flexing of the muscles. This skill can become crucial when dealing with a customer as it makes it easier for the person practicing NLP to determine the type of effect that they are having on other people.

This will help the person practicing NLP to stop when they have achieved their desired outcome from the other person.

FTake for example, you are working in the sales department of a busy clothes store. A customer walks in and you notice that they have broken a small sweat, are a little out of breath and keep glancing at their watch even before they have started shopping.

If you have been using the techniques in NLP, you might conclude that the customer is in a hurry and needs to be served quickly to ensure they make their next appointment. Therefore, you are able to adjust the level of service that you are offering accordingly.

c) Change your behavior to ensure an outcome
This ties in directly with the first principle, and really addresses the core of NLP, which is behavior modification. In a business setting, you need to be flexible enough to change gears if you notice that the reaction you expect is not the one you are getting.

This can only work efficiently if you always ensure that you have your end goal in your mind. This is particularly true if you used the power of visualization and had a picture the steps that you need to take to meet your goal.

To measure the response, tap into your skill as explained in the second principle. Should you be achieving you desired outcome, you should continue with your pre-determined course of action. If, however, you are not meeting your desired outcome, you should attempt to use another approach.
When you spend time reviewing or watching your behavior, you can easily save time and anguish by simply being aware of the emotions and how you can deal with them.

d) Taking Action
This calls for actively using NLP to make decisions in the present moment. There is no point in taking time to learn all the NLP techniques if you do not put you're your learning to the test.

The thing is when working towards changing behavior; it is important to do things in the present. By being present, it becomes easier to modify and improve behavior where necessary.

Companies that send their staff on training for NLP skills, especially practitioner skills, will often focus on only sending their management team with the assumption that they would have learnt a new skill which can then trickle down to the rest of the team.

NLP is not a tool that should be limited to the management within in a business. Rather, it is a technology that everyone in the organization should be well versed with in order to ensure adequate fulfillment of the organizational objectives. Employees can use NLP techniques to reach their optimum performance levels or to communicate better with the customers.

When one uses NLP skills in dealing with customers or communicating internally, the result is often quite clear – a percentage increase in spending by customers or in productivity of the employees.

When an employee at any level is trained to learn NLP skills, they become significantly empowered which usually leads to their increased output. NLP will teach each employee to create, comprehend and apply anything that can be done on a mental map.

In business, the aforementioned points highlight what the most common business challenge is. The main challenge is proper communication. Communication includes what goes on in a company, as well as what is happening with the customers.

Becoming the Most Influential Person You Know
When you downloaded this book, you have that desire to master the art of influencing others. You would learn how to do so as long as you understand and practice influential and persuasive language. This is the language that people leaders use in order to actually empower others and help them develop themselves. Yes, using neuro- linguistic programming is geared to also helping other people around you. It is made to help you help others see that they can change the way they behave in order to achieve goals. It is not a selfish endeavor, but rather, it is driven by your desire to make others feel that you are achieving a common goal, and they should believe in it the same way that you do. That would enable you to present them what is good in what you offer them. For this reason, the techniques in this chapter would allow you to convince others that you would help them get the results that they want.

Become the Expert
In order to become the most influential person in a group, you first

have to establish that you are the subject matter expert. That means that there is no other person that they can reach out to as of the moment when it comes to knowing what they need. For example, if you are trying to sell them headphones, you have to convince them that you have been using a lot of other headphones, and that you are actually trained to know what good quality sound is. Of course, as an expert, you also have the ability to provide them everything that they need to know about what a good pair of headphones really is, in the way that they can understand,

But here comes the good part – in order to become a real expert that they can count on, especially when it comes to business, you have to use a specific kind of language that actually makes them feel that they made a decision. If they decided to buy what you are selling, you have to make them feel that they made the best decision that they can do at that moment. You do this with the understanding that people are not stupid – they want to feel that they made a decision not because they are forced to. When it comes to being a person that can get repeat customers, it does not pay to be pushy. Nobody likes a manipulative salesperson. Nobody would like to work under a coercive boss.

At this point, you realize that you are not actually forcing them to buy from you or make an agreement that is favorable to you. You are simply just suggesting that they make a choice, and you make them see that is not for your benefit, but theirs. However, the bottom line is, they are the ones who are going to make the choice, according to your predictions. When you think about it, it is very similar to how some card tricks work – people may think that they have picked a card that the magician would never guess, but of course, the other thing happened instead. By using the power of suggestion, you would always be able to "read" what is going on in the other person's mind. However, the reality is, you influence the other person to do that action. At the same time, you have to assume that people already know what they want – all they need to do is to find the best way to lead them to that.

Magic Tricks
Card magicians and mentalists follow the similar rules of NLP – they use the ability to instill certain programming to another person, and with their body and verbal language, direct the audience to look at what they want to see, which is magic. NLP is similar to sleight of hand – you create a scenario about you and your activity, and then you tell say that in such manner that others can have a vivid impression of that in their minds. If you are a magician, you want to tell say that scenario in a very subtle way, because that would of course, give away your trick. Nevertheless, if you were trying to sell something, you would want to keep how you convinced others to.

Here's a thing about trying to control the actions of others, or at least pretending that you can predict what they are going to do next – you have to be very visual when it comes to directing them what they should do next. If you want a person to choose any letter in the alphabet, and make sure that it coincides with the one that you want them to choose, you have to subliminally influence them to think about that letter before they make a choice. How do you do that? If you want to make them pick the letter A, you can place an apple inside the room where they can see it at the corner of their eye, or you may ask a person inside the same room to wear a shirt with A printed on the front.

You may not have thought about this before, but this is also the secret of advertisements, or at least, the very effective ones. You can convince people to make a choice depending on the series of commands that you require them to do in order to make the choice that fits your purpose. More often than not, the choices that people make are those that are logical according to their senses – if you make them see dark-colored water in a bottle, and then you place them in a hot room, they may tell you that they want cola. The choices that people make are often sensory, and when prompted to make a choice, they will choose something that conforms to their experience.

Chapter 14 – New Education

As one considers the purpose of NLP (which is helping people to understand and take control of their thoughts and feelings for a positive change), it becomes apparent why NLP has such an important role to play in education.

Learning to use NLP techniques while still a student can greatly affect how you conduct yourself in a business - in a very positive way. This is because, as a student, you use NLP to figure out the way that you learn. Learning occurs in three primary learning styles categories which are explained as follows.

a) Visual Learning

This is where the student learns the most and responds positively to visual stimuli. These include demonstrations, charts, reading and videos.

A student who learns visually will face a challenge when it comes to memorizing information or reading notes through a text book. If they have pictures that they can piece together in their minds, they are more likely to learn what is being taught.

Students who prefer visual learning are the type that are is likely to come up with brainstorming sessions, featuring a visual representation of an entire idea.

The vVisuals are excellent because they provide a new way to see things. Practicing visualization involves looking into the future and picturing an achievableed goal. This technique also fits within visual learning and can powerfully replace limiting beliefs in the students.

b) Auditory Learning

In this type of learning, a student prefers to learn by having things explained to them in detail. This knowledge is important to be aware of when one goes back to working with students because it may determine whether one has a leader or a follower in their classroom.

Learning through awaiting explanation is excellent for students who have to learn and understand the step by step processes. These students are able to remember everything that they are being taught, because the system fits in with the way that they remember and assimilate information. If for any reason these students are taught using visual aids, for example, they might have some difficult in keeping up or following the path that the information is leading them to.

A follower, in this case, would simplye use this way of learning to receive instructions and would then follow themn without question.

The reason for this is that as long as the instructions are followed exactly, there can be no negative or wrong results. The student would be safe from making mistakes.

A leader would have a different outcome when using this learning technique. After the words have been explained, a leader could choose to take ownership of these words. If they have been stated in the negative, they can be approached as a positive. A student who is able to do make this change in approaches has the ability to reframe, and this is a positive result that comes about when one practices NLP actively.

c) Kinetic Learning
In this type of learning, the student will learn the best when they carry out an activity on their own. This is particularly true for taking part in experiments or other classes that have a practical aspect.

The best thing to do, in this case, would be to give the student a set of instructions and leave them to follow them the best way they can. In between, one can check on the student and point them in the right direction should it appear that things are not being done according to plan.

Students who prefer this type of independent learning will display short attention spans when they have to listen to long lectures or lessons. They prefer short, direct presentations of ideas, and they have beening given the opportunity to execute these ideas on their own.

The aforementioned learning style categories are ideal for students. However, NLP can also be highly beneficial for teachers. By taking the time to understand the different learning styles of each student, the teacher is then equipped with the tools to adopt tried and tested methods to help the students do well and have all their educational needs met.
This chapter can also be applied to trying to understand the way other people, such as customers, perceive things. With this skill, it will be much easier to handle them with care.

Chapter 15: Parenting Positively

When one becomes a parent, they are filled with joy and expectation and then as their child grows older, they begin to realize something new. That they need to learn and understand the emotions and feelings of their child in such a way that they can have a positive effect on their development.

One of the best ways to do this is to find a way to view the world through the child's eyes, communicating more deeply and fulfilling all the child's emotional needs.

To start, this chapter shall look at NLP throughout five senses which make up our external territory. These five senses are sight, hearing, smell, touch and taste. All of these will form part of a memory.

What happens with children is that they take this external territory and give it an internal representation, known as the map. They then view the entire world through this map, with their perceptions, beliefs and values creating filters that they look through. These filters and the children's own perceptions are what make them unique individuals.

Through the Eyes of a Child

Parents can use the techniques and tools of NLP to look at the world through the eyes of their child. NLP helps a parent see what the child is seeingsees, feel what they are feeling and hear what they are hearing. With this knowledge, a parent is better equipped to steer their children in the right direction.

This skill can be practically applied to trying to help your child overcome a fear. By seeing things forom the child's point of view, a parent can reduce their fear to nothing.

If you are trying to improve the communication between yourself and your child, NLP is an excellent option to try. By being positive with your child and communicating clearly, you are likely to get the same responses from your child. In essence, they will mirror your behavior and emotional state.

Take, for example, a case where you are trying to discipline a child. Your natural instinct would be to correct them and with a negative, such as, do not throw your toys. The likely result will be more instances where the toys get thrown. If you are parenting using NLP techniques as your guide, rather than speaking in the negative, you will discipline your child from a positive angle. Therefore, you are more likely to say be careful which will actually have the child being more cautious and trying to keep their toys safe.

You can also teach your child to use some NLP skills so that they can build their confidence as they construct the map of their worlds. You can start by teaching your children how to visualize so that they can succeed in school. Picturing a positive outcome may encourage them to concentrate more when they are in class. You could also slowly teach them NLP techniques that they can use to handle difficult situations.

Teaching Children NLP Skills

By giving your children the benefits of NLP techniques, you are helping them acquire good habits, get excellent communication skills and develop their very own high levels of confidence. This will be of substantial help to them as they move into the future.

As mentioned earlier, communication is key when parenting and by adopting NLP techniques, you cannot not communicate. NLP requires you to be conscious ofn your nonverbal communication, just as much as your verbal communication. This ensures that you do not send conflicting messages to your child, where what you say does not match the actions that you are making.

Sending conflicting actions might occur when one is telling their child "I love you", yet their facial expressions shows frustration or their teeth are clenched. This means that the child is getting a positive message, yet is being busy giving out a negative message using body language.

NLP demands that one remains present, which stops a parent from reacting to a child's past behavior or a memory of something that the child did. As parents, being human, one may shout loudly at your child as the upset has gathered within you. As the child may not be able to see directly in front of them, they would react to a past event can lead to confusion, and also misunderstanding or unhappiness. So it is important to note your tone of voice, the volume that you are speaking at and the actions that you are making.

Remember that you can interpret the meaning of your communication by observing the way your child responds. If you can see that your message is being misunderstood or getting lost in translation, you need to change the message that you are giving forward.

NLP opens these doors for you, revealing the options that exist for improved communication. You may have a child who learns visually, so it may be easier to communicate with them by using pictures or other visual aids.

Finally, without a doubt, children will try to push your boundaries. In an attempt to get the attention of a parent, some children will resort to displaying bad or negative behavior, such as being rude, violent and lashing out.

As a parent, one can use NLP techniques to control how to react to these situations. The idea here is to react as positively as possibley. Therefore, when faced with a rude child, give a positive reaction which is called a pattern interrupt.

By reacting positively, your child will also feel the need to control their reactions and diffuse the situation.

Chapter 16: Persuasiveness Using Conversational Hypnosis

Conversational hypnosis is one of NLP's most widely used techniques. This technique takes **full advantage of the power ofr language.** The conscious use of language achieves several goals that will eventually lead up to you being able to persuade your listener. To use the language, you can choose from a combination of several language frames: agreement, purpose, backtrack and contrast.

When you use language to achieve a communication goal, use these language frames. The **agreement frame** means that you accept and recognize your listener's point of view. By agreeing with him, you strengthen your rapport. **Purpose** means you look for the motivation behind the listener on why he does or does not perform an action. **Backtrack** means you take notice of topics that are not relevant and return your listener to the track of the conversation. **Contrast** means that you show him other possibilities if the topic of the persuasion is not done.

For example, you are selling a product to your listener, note the following conversation:

Listener: The price is too high (your listener's opinion)

You: Yes, I know that but the benefits more than make up for the price (agreement)
Listener: I am not sure but I would need to check with my family first (your listener's influencer)

You: I agree, your family will more than enjoy this product, they will also benefit with it like you will (motivation)

Listener: The product sounds good but I am quite busy in at work and I have a deadline to attend to (veering off the topic)

You: Yes, you are right the product is good and this is why your decision of purchasing it will also be good (backtrack). In fact, without this product, you can end up with the following problems (contrast)

Another important lesson to be gained from NLP is the laws of influence. These are:

1. Reciprocation. This means that you imply to your client that the same way you get something out of the deal, he get also gets something of equal or more value. For example, "I am sure you know that

I will get something out of this deal. The least I can do is to make you get more out of this deal."

2. Social Proof. It is important to show your listener that other people like him also made a decision. For example, "Your coworkers also made the decisions to purchase and I can even tell you that they are more than willing to share with you the benefits of this product."

3. Authority. Aside from the fact that your listener's peers also made the decision, credibility can also be given by mentioning an authority figure that endorses the decision. For example, "This may sound boring to you but I want to give you statistics and research findings that prove that the product does what it claims to do."

4. Scarcity. This is when you imply that what you offer cannot be accessed by everyone and your client is one of the few who can. This also creates a sense of urgency. "Each area is only given a certain amount to sell because the company wants to gain more ground. This is why the quantity I can offer my clients is limited."

5. Commitment. This means that you need to follow through with the persuasion and the conversation. This will show to your listener that you give value to his decision. For example, "I really understand the dilemma you are in right now, I was there too but the same way I was helped along the way, I want to extend that to you also."

A majority of NLP trainees belong to careers that take full advantage of the power of persuasion, such as in sales and marketing. These language frames create a solid foundation that can guide them in addressing the concerns of their clients. It also proves to be of vital use to negotiators who want to make the best out of the deal.

Conversational hypnosis cannot be done overnight even with full knowledge of the technique. Try practicing it with a colleague before you roll it out to your clients. Since communication can also be done both verbally and non-verbally, consider recording yourself to both hear both your words and see your body language.

Chapter 17: Self-Belief & Confidence Using Future Pacing

Future pacing involves the use of effective visual imagery. It is meant to verify if the change that is expected in a person is already in place after an intervention. To verify, an image is developed that represents the changes in the look, behavior and feeling of a person that is reflective of a successful intervention. After the intervention, the look, behavior and feeling of the person must be similar to the developed image. If it is not, then it means the intervention is unsuccessful.

Another use of future pacing is to allow the person to feel the result of the intervention **even before** the intervention is completed. The idea behind this is that the image will act as a motivation towards the person to become successful in the intervention. The image will also become a guide for the person on how to look, behave or feel. NLP further asserts that when the current state and the future image are always put together, the person can no longer differentiate between his current and future state, therefore the developed image **merges** into the person.

Self-belief and confidence are some of the most highly desired characteristics that every person tries to achieve. It can be used to propel you towards achieving your goals by making you more assertive with others and more at ease with yourself. The fFuture pacing technique can help in developing this important trait for you. This technique will prove to be useful, especially for those who regularly have feelings of self-doubt.

First, set aside at least an hour where you can be alone in a quiet room. Make sure that there are no distractions. If you are adept in meditating, you can make use of your meditation techniques to put you in a calm and contemplative but focused state. Picture yourself in your mind in your most ideal and most confident state.

Begin by assessing the image and ask yourself these questions, what do you look like? How is your skin? What is your weight?

What are you wearing? How do you smell? How is your posture? How do you move? What gestures do you use? How do you walk? What are your facial expressions? How do you speak? What is the tone, speed and volume of your voice? How do you introduce yourself to new people? How do you talk with other people? What are you doing while with a group of friends, family or colleagues? How do you interact with your boss and your subordinates?

You can ask more questions as you like, it is important to make the image as vivid as possible. Keep painting the picture in your mind with as much details as you can. If you have time left, you can document your image. If you are good with drawing, you can sketch your image. If not, you can use words to describe the image of yourself.

Now that you have the future and self-confident image of yourself, start by merging one characteristic at a time. You can start with the easiest and most superficial, such as clothing. Move forward with the way you stand, walk and sit. Next, mimic the way your future image speaks. Continue with the rest of the image on your own pace. You will eventually merge your current self with your future image.

Chapter 18: The Value of Neuro-Linguistic Programming

"As long as you believe it is impossible, you will actually never find out if it is possible or not."
John Seymour

Neuro Linguistic Programming can be used for self development in all kinds of areas, from becoming spiritual right through to being able to help kids grow in their understanding of life. It can be used to help people aim higher and to give sportsmen and women more impetus in reaching beyond their goals, rather than having set goals which place a limitation on their potential.

Such is the scope of Neuro-Linguistic Programming that it can also be used for developing friendships and developing "self" in a case where self esteem is low. It is used in psychology and helps people overcome many of the problems associated with perceptions, beliefs, doubts and negativity. When the system was developed as a philosophy, little was known about the scope to which this system could be applied. Over the past half a century, the opening up of different areas has been very valuable to business people and individuals alike.

In a world where multitasking and spreading oneself thin over a plethora of activities have become all the rage, a program like NLP, scientifically devised and tested for optimum results, takes a front seat when it comes to self-development and improvement of one's own brain and its capacities. In this chapter, we will explore how the techniques involved in the NLP program can be best utilized and exploited in order to reap maximum benefits out of it.

Like most ideologies implemented in life, NLP practitioners believe that it is not WHAT you do that brings you success, but HOW you do it. Irrespective of the nature of the job being done, if done with 100% efficiency guarantees optimum results. The sStructure takes priority over content, and heavy focus is laid on getting the job done with minimum effort, maximum efficiency and optimum time.

NLP teaches us to quit worrying about making money, and instead divert all the energy spent into that towards more fruitful activities such as long term planning, analyzing how money can be efficiently invested, recognizing and opening themselves to opportunities and honing the skills needed to identify great investments.

The common man will perceive money as being the sole trouble in his life, and will thereby treat himself as a victim to the trap of money.

However, with the help of NLP, we can re-model our thinking so that we are no longer the victim in this rat race, and change a certain view we might hold in our mind about ourselves. When we imagine ourselves to be helpless, we are effectively ensuring in generating a mindset which will further promote and cultivate deep rooted feelings of helplessness, in turn fulfilling the unconscious's prediction of becoming helpless. This is what is known as a "vicious cycle".

However, when we apply the concepts of NLP and channelize our mind to think in a particular direction about us, we learn how to control our thought process. We are also able to clearly perceive and recognize obvious money making schemes, giving us the courage needed to take the risk and hence reach out for chances which money may provide. As NLP has designed the mid to turn any digging field into a mine of opportunities, three states of the mind, therefore engage in ensuring that any decision taken with regards to money is implemented with the highest level of accuracy and precision, hence ensuring excellent results.

Seasoned veterans in the practice of employing the techniques of NLP to money making confide that all that is required is a change from the negative mindset associated with money, to a more positive one, where new ideas are embraced and welcomed. Negative beliefs and thoughts about money need to be avoided in order for the NLP to work. Apart from this, it isn't just about seeing yourself in a rich position. It also helps to find out how people in influential and higher positions handle their money, as well as the attitude they adopt when dealing with money. Money should be regarded as the natural counterpart of building business relationships and offering services to wealthy people.

Once the human mind has been trained to perceive money as a stepping stone for success, and not as a weak link to failure, it can be conditioned to analyze the different methods and measures which can be taken to amplify the money which one has in one's hands into larger, enormous amounts. NLP also incorporates a sense of being better able to handle earned money. As is often the case, many times people who earn huge amounts blow it all away, by not being resourceful and practicing sustained spending. This is a downward spiral, which sucks out all enthusiasm and effort needed to maintain a streak of positivity with respect to money making. NLP conditions the mind to implement wise, well thought out expenditure plans, and carrying out savings plans also becomes a much easier task when coupled with the norms laid down by the NLP program.

Once all this has been achieved, money management comes into the picture. The instinct which tells you whether to invest in a particular project, or whether running a risk of losing some money to make a profit out of it later on is worthwhile, such instincts can be honed and perfected with the help of the NLP techniques. As explained before, NLP trains the mind to dwell deep into the unconscious to help in improving the accuracy of these instincts and better the predictability of a situation.

As you can see now, there are various methods and tricks which can be implemented, all parts of the NLP program, which will forever change the way you look at and think about money. Once this happens, the sky is the limit. However, there are a few precautions needed to be taken to ensure that desired results are achieved

The individuals who take a course in Neuro Linguistic Programming will usually start their course with skepticism and teachers have been quoted as saying that they arrive with all of their past baggage, their doubts, their problems and that the first day of a Neuro Linguistic Programming course is always the most amusing from the perspective of teachers. This isn't in a mean sense. It is because those teachers know that by the end of the course, those students will go home with a richer sense of self, a more complete perspective of the world around them and that it will be almost as if a weight has been taken from their shoulders.
The potential of the mind is explored and students learn that the unconscious messages the brain is capable of processing gives them a reserve that they never thought possible. Students enthuse about their courses and become more positive and able to see their own potential more clearly, without placing boundaries on their possibilities.

What you learn from courses on Neuro Linguistic Programming is now to deal with life's surprises and not be phased by unexpected happenings. You learn how to understand others better and thus relate to them in a more open manner. You gain information on how to impress people without even really trying and finding an inner happiness that isn't easily achieved and that is long lasting.

Lecturers are taught about incorporating a certain amount of humor into their teaching so that students can easily relate to the situations being explained. This humor helps to show the levity that people feel once they know the tools of Neuro Linguistic Programming and incorporate them into their lives.

Looking to find your spiritual self? Then Neuro-Linguistic Programming could take you one step nearer to becoming your ultimate best, at one with your belief and able ability to lead by example.

The benefits of this kind of training are so many that it would be impossible to list them all. However, whatever walk of life you find yourself in, you will gain something from the courses and come away feeling much more aware of your own potential for success.

One way to describe what NLP does is that it fills the gap in everyone's education. Through schools, we learn all of the reading, writing and arithmetic subjects. We learn art, science, biology, history and the necessary subjects that will help us in our journey through life. Career wise, people need this standard education to help them to qualify for jobs later on. What NLP does is filling in the gaps in our education and give us food for thought on behavior patterns, thought sequences and mood enhancement. All of these help to make human beings more complete and thus able to give more to their everyday lives.

Chapter 19: Things You Must Remember in Using NLP

Since there are no harmful effects to the NLP, it is expected that some side effects will present themselves over the course of the method. However, this is not the case. But a few precautionary measures need to be taken nevertheless when dabbling with NLP, which prevent the plan from going awry resulting in disastrous end outputs.

• As the foundation for the program rests on the concept of comparison, it is important to not go overboard by over estimating other people or undermining one's own capacities, as this leads to a complete derailment of the purpose of the program. Holding oneself on a high pedestal can also have derogative effects, as self-criticism is an important feedback review measure for any self-development scheme.

• NLP primarily focuses on the control of emotions, and feelings through controlling measures. NLP helps in achieving focus and organization, by controlling emotions and actions. However, this must done within limits, as a complete lack of emotions will make a person cold and insensitive and spoil one's relations and connections with people. Overusing them or displaying them in inappropriate situations hinders progress, and thus needs to be avoided. Be the boss of your mind, don't let it boss you.

• Focus is key to getting results out of the program, so it is imperative to have a clear goal in mind before beginning. Goals may be altered, as mentioned before, however, too many alterations can lead to a confused and befuddled mind. Once a goal has been set, try to focus on achieving the goal in its original form, rather than modifying it according to your whims. NLP is a scientific program, functioning on analysis of facts, and as such should be approached as one.

• Do NOT expect results on the very first day of the program. The NLP program works according to one's capabilities and the time taken for results to be exhibited varies from person to person, as each human is wired differently. Hence, raising your expectations might lead to disappointments and a diminishing enthusiasm, which could prove disastrous for mind control. Shortcut methods and distractions need to be avoided at all costs, as this will only further hinder the progress of the program

Conclusion

If you have never been creative in your life and you were suddenly told that it was possible to be creative, you would probably dismiss this thought because your mind is programmed to believe that you are not creative. Tap into the subconscious and learn how much creativity lurks within that place you underestimate. It's amazing where this journey will take you.

Grab a notebook and a pen and set aside quality time each day to do this for yourself. You can work NLP technique into any schedule and see positive results pretty fast. Each step is easy to understand and do. Before you know it you can have the problem isolated and put a plan of action in place that creates the lasting change you desire.

There are many types of behavior modification therapy available. They all work to some degree, but it is the time and expense involved that can be frustrating. Most traditional behavior modification therapies include time-intensive programs that cost you and your insurance company a lot of money over time. NLP works the same way, but it brings you to the results faster without the expense.

If you have some behaviors that you would like to change or want to enjoy a more stable emotional well-being NLP offers you all of the benefits of intense therapy without the hassle and high cost. You now have all of the tools at your access to get started right away. Make this the day that you finally took control of your life and got the edge!

Use empathy and learn how empathy works to communicate with others by suggestion rather than by giving definite answers that cut other people's hopes and dreams down in size. There is no need to belittle. In fact, you grow richer from learning to use empathy because you become a better person for it and are able to make friendships that benefit everyone involved.

Learn not to limit yourself by believing in things that are limiting in themselves. An example recently read was where a person believed that birds all have feathers. It's something that limits the believer, since by that premise penguins would be excluded. What NLP does is help you to see a much bigger picture that doesn't limit what you see and that's when your life begins to take on a whole new meaning.

It is hoped that this book has opened your mind to the possibility of taking your learning processes further on the subject of NLP. You will be very glad that you did, as the techniques briefly outlined in this book, have vast potential.

Did You Like The Real Mind Control?

Before you go, we'd like to say "thank you" for purchasing our book. So a big thanks for downloading this book and reading all the way to the end. Now we'd like ask for a *small* favour. Could you please take a minute or two and leave a review for this book on Amazon

This feedback will help us continue writing this kind of books. And if you loved it, then please let me know.

Leave a review for this book on Amazon by searching for the title,

The Real Mind Control

Want to read more exciting stories for FREE?

Join my **V.I.P** List now!

I regularly GIVEAWAY FREE books and SPECIAL DISCOUNTS!

Join my mailing list and be one of thousands we already receiving FREEBIES!

Join by visiting this site:

http://www.ravenspress.com/freeselfhelp/

Or Scan this QR Code from your smartphone to go the website directly